"Marissa Nehlsen masterfully transforms traditional financial advice into a profound life strategy. *Live Life Rich* is more than monetary guidance—it's an actionable blueprint for personal transformation."
>—Kelly Resendez, EVP of GoodLeap,
>cofounder of Gobundance Women, bestselling
>author, and international speaker

"*Live Life Rich* is a master class in financial clarity, empowerment, and purpose-driven success. This book is the ultimate roadmap to abundance."
>—Joanne Hession, founder and CEO of LIFT Ireland

"If you've ever dreamed of achieving financial freedom while staying true to your purpose, *Live Life Rich* is your master class—read it and live it!"
>—Jason Thomas, PhD, CFA, professional investor,
>and founder of one of the fastest-growing
>investment management firms in the US

"Marissa's genuine care for your success shines through on every page, lifting you with her wisdom and encouragement."
>—The Gardiner Brothers, five-time world champion
>dancers, content creators, and speakers

"A powerful fusion of motivation, inspiration, and actionable strategy. *Live Life Rich* is more than just a guide to achieving wealth—it's a blueprint for lasting success, fulfillment, and purpose."
>—Dana Burkhardt, vice president and head of
>business consulting of AssetMark, Inc.

"If you're looking to build financial freedom without sacrificing your core values, *Live Life Rich* is a must-read."
>—Lauren Johnson, performance psychology
>advisor, coach, and speaker

"I can't even begin to tell you how much I've learned about finances from Marissa Nehlsen. She's changed my thinking—which is changing my results. You need to read this book!"
—Charlie Wetzel, writing partner with John Maxwell and author of *Answer the Call: Developing the Writer Within You*

"Marissa provides a transformative roadmap that bridges the gap between transactional success and meaningful wealth creation."
—Dr. Eric Peoples, keynote speaker, executive leadership educator, CEO, and founder

"Keep turning pages, and you will keep finding keys to financial freedom. Marissa serves as a master guide to abundance—without all the unnecessary baggage!"
—Joshua Finley, speaker, author, and coach

"If you've ever wondered how to turn financial chaos into clarity and control, *Live Life Rich* will guide you every step of the way."
—Daniela Nica, entrepreneur, founder of MentorMind Method & Braindology, and cognitive scientist

"Marissa's tax strategies are something every person should know. With her profound wisdom, she simplifies the most effective financial strategies—everyone should read this."
—Kelly Price, entrepreneur and servant leader

"If you've ever dreamed of achieving financial freedom while staying true to your purpose, *Live Life Rich* is the book for you. Marissa breaks down complex ideas into actionable insights that can transform your business and life."
—Dianna Kokoszka, entrepreneur, author, speaker, investor, former CEO of Keller Williams International Realty MAPS Coaching and Training, and current CEO of Dynamic Growth Collective, DKBusinesses, and Coaching Consortium

LIVE LIFE
RICH

THE ENTREPRENEUR'S GUIDE
to Dream Big, Multiply Your Money, and Take Control of Your Financial Freedom

MARISSA NEHLSEN

Live Life Rich: The Entrepreneur's Guide to Dream Big, Multiply Your Money, and Take Control of Your Financial Freedom
Copyright © 2025 by Marissa Nehlsen

All rights reserved. No part of this publication may be reproduced, stored in a retrieval system, or transmitted in any form by any means, electronic, mechanical, photocopy, recording, or otherwise, without the prior permission of the publisher, except as provided by USA copyright law.

No patent liability is assumed with respect to the use of the information contained herein. Although every precaution has been taken in the preparation of this book, the publisher and author assume no responsibility for errors or omissions. Neither is any liability assumed for damages resulting from the use of the information contained herein.

This book is intended for informational purposes only. It is not intended to be used as the sole basis for financial or investing decisions, nor should it be construed as advice designed to meet the particular needs of an individual's situation.

Scripture quotations taken from The Holy Bible, New International Version® NIV® Copyright © 1973, 1978, 1984, 2011 by Biblica, Inc.® Used with permission. All rights reserved worldwide.

Published by Maxwell Leadership Publishing, an imprint of Forefront Books, Nashville, Tennessee.
Distributed by Simon & Schuster.

Library of Congress Control Number: 2025906082

Print ISBN: 979-8-88710-041-8
E-book ISBN: 979-8-88710-042-5

Cover Design by George Stevens, G Sharp Design LLC
Interior Design by PerfecType, Nashville, TN

Printed in the United States of America

25 26 27 28 29 30 [LSC] 10 9 8 7 6 5 4 3 2 1

To the amazing JaJaCon, aka my mother, Connie Philipenko. You taught me how to be victorious and never a victim. You showed me how to live out love and to lead my life with faith, knowing that I am always enough and never too much, and that I can do all things through Christ who strengthens me. Thank you for being a model, a guide, and an incredible light in my life and in the lives of so many.

I also dedicate this book to every warrior-spirit entrepreneur who desires and works daily to live life rich. If just one life breathes easier today because you exist—you have lived a rich life. Well done.

CONTENTS

Foreword by John C. Maxwell   9
Start Here: You Are More Than Enough and Never Too Much   11

1. When the Vision Is Clear, the Decisions Are Easy   23
2. Prepare or Repair: Your Freedom Plan   37
3. Assemble Your Freedom Team   57
4. The Art of the Introduction   77
5. Make Money Your Best Employee   95
6. 8 Streams of Income Every Entrepreneur Should Consider   111
7. Fire Your Worst Business Partner: The Tax Collector   125
8. Will You Pass on a Mess or a Masterpiece?   157
9. 13 Money Habits to Create Wealth   211
10. The World Needs You Rich   223

Acknowledgments   233
About the Author   237
Notes   239

FOREWORD

The greatest reward for a leader is to see others succeed. And that is exactly what Marissa Nehlsen does every day. She has been a dream maker for countless people, and through this book, she's going to do the same for you.

I've had the privilege of knowing Marissa for many years. In all my years, I have met few people with the same level of financial wisdom as her. Her journey from a passionate entrepreneur to a powerhouse business leader has been nothing short of inspirational. As a Maxwell Leadership Certified Coach, Marissa has not only embraced the principles we've championed but also elevated them with her unique vision and relentless drive.

If you asked me today, "What book should I read to get the highest ROI?" I would name this very book. In *Live Life Rich*, Marissa has designed a comprehensive road map to help entrepreneurs and business owners navigate the complexities of achieving true financial freedom and fulfillment. In these pages, you will discover a clear vision for business, finances, and life, making your complex decisions easier and more manageable.

Through Marissa's guidance, you'll learn how to make money work for you, ensure its preservation, and multiply it effectively. Marissa addresses essential aspects of financial planning—from minimizing tax burdens and safeguarding against common pitfalls to building a robust network and preparing a lasting legacy. Her advice is practical and actionable, rooted in real-world experience, and designed to help you achieve the freedom and fulfillment you seek. Another way to put it—she leaves no stone unturned.

Marissa's not just sharing theories; she's offering battle-tested strategies that have helped her and countless others achieve financial freedom and business success. Her ability to simplify complex financial concepts and present them in a relatable, actionable manner is truly remarkable.

As someone who has witnessed Marissa's journey firsthand, I can attest to her authenticity and dedication. She's not just a leader; she's a visionary who genuinely cares about helping others succeed. This book is a reflection of her life's work and her unwavering belief that with the right mindset and strategies, anyone can achieve financial freedom and live a rich, fulfilling life.

Whether you're a seasoned entrepreneur or just starting on your business journey, say hello to your new life of freedom. Marissa Nehlsen has laid out the path—now it's up to you to take the first step.

Warmest regards,
John C. Maxwell
#1 *New York Times* bestselling author, founder of Maxwell Leadership

START HERE
You Are More Than Enough and Never Too Much

Money. What does that little five-letter word mean to you? What kind of emotions, memories, and stories does it stir up for you?

For most, money and fear go hand in hand. Fear of not having enough, fear of losing it, fear of failing to keep up with others. I don't think I need to be an expert in psychology or human behavior to tell you that operating or relating to anything primarily through fear is not going to result in much good, especially if you want more of it.

If fear doesn't dominate our thoughts about money, then we've at least grown up with mixed messages about it. Some of us were taught that money is the ultimate measure of success, while others were taught it's the root of all evil. One of the biggest traps in life, especially in the world of money, is comparison. We're constantly comparing ourselves to others—people who seem to have more, live better, achieve faster. Social media makes this even worse. We see the highlight reels of other people's lives, and it's easy to feel like we're falling short. We believe that more money will bring us more love, fun, or meaning. To some extent that may be true. Taking your loved ones on a dream vacation, buying nice things, or building schools by donating to charity can totally enrich your life.

But no amount of money can ever quell your fears until you learn to accept and love yourself for who you are. See, money can buy a roof over your head, put food on your table, and provide for you and your loved ones. But it can't fill the deeper voids in your life. It won't heal broken relationships, give you a deeper sense of purpose, or quiet the inner critic who tells you you're not enough. Money solves money problems—and rarely anything more or anything less.

I remember the moment this really hit home for me. I was sitting in my house, a beautiful place I had bought after my divorce, furnished with all new things. I had a glass of red wine in my hand, surrounded by what looked like success. But despite everything, I felt empty. I had gone through a divorce, my kids were struggling, and I was alone. Money alone couldn't solve those problems. It couldn't fix the pain inside me or bring back what I had lost.

It's important to talk about this before we dive headlong into this journey together because if we don't define and improve our relationship with money, more of it will not help. I like to say that for most of us, especially entrepreneurs, our relationship with money is kind of like texting someone who has no interest in you. You know the feeling—you send a perfectly crafted message, full of charm, wit, maybe even a little vulnerability, and then . . . nothing. Crickets.

You sit there, staring at your phone, thinking, *Maybe they're just busy.* So you try again, putting even more effort into it. You work overtime, sacrifice weekends, skip meals (OK, maybe not meals), all in the name of "hustling." But what does money do? It leaves you on "Read." It teases you with just enough to keep you hooked but never quite delivers the full commitment you're after.

You chase it, flatter it, rearrange your whole schedule to accommodate it, and it still ghosts you at the end of the month. Worse, it has no problem popping up unexpectedly—usually when you're least prepared—demanding attention, like, *Oh, hey, you need new tires, and by the way, your taxes are due.* You bend over backward trying to make it happy, but no matter how hard you work, it always feels like you're the one doing all the chasing, while money's out there playing hard to get. I know I can't be the only one who has felt this way.

That said, it's not wrong to want more money, because how you use it determines whether it serves you or controls you. So, what if money isn't something to fear, worship, or chase? What if, instead of being the destination, it's simply a tool?

When you look at money this way, it becomes less about what you've got and more about what you can do with it. Now, you may say, "That's easy for you, Marissa. You have money!" Actually, the lessons in this book are ones I learned before I got to a place of financial freedom. I truly believe that learning these lessons are why I was able to reach and surpass my goals.

Business is one of the greatest personal, spiritual, and emotional development tools we have. It forces us to grow, to face our fears, and to stretch beyond what we thought we were capable of. I want to touch on something that many entrepreneurs experience but rarely talk about: you can be great at business and still feel like you've got a hole in your boat. You might excel at growing your business, closing sales, or marketing yourself, but if you don't have a plan for managing your money, it will eventually catch up with you.

I've seen this time and time again with entrepreneurs who are incredibly talented in their fields. They're bringing in revenue, sometimes substantial amounts, but somehow, the money seems to disappear. It slips through the cracks because they don't have the financial systems or discipline in place to ensure that their money works for them, not the other way around.

Business acumen and money acumen aren't the same thing. You can have all the business savvy in the world, but if you don't develop the skills to manage, invest, and grow your money, you'll always feel like you're running uphill. We'll explore how to build those money systems and habits so that the financial success you achieve in your business is sustainable and aligned with your personal goals. Because no matter how good you are at your craft, if you don't take control of your money, it will take control of you.

As you read through this book, you'll notice that I speak to entrepreneurs at various stages of their journey. The truth is, regardless of where you are, financial and business planning require a deep understanding of your unique situation. Entrepreneurs come in all shapes and sizes, and your approach to managing and growing your business will vary depending on the phase you're in.

For those of you just starting out, building a business can feel both exciting and daunting. You may be a solopreneur, working from your kitchen table, or perhaps you've just hired your first team member. At this stage, the focus is on figuring out how to get clients, generate consistent income, and manage your cash flow. You may still be finding your voice in the market or testing which products and services resonate most with your target audience. I'll cover some broad strategies to help you establish the foundational elements that will allow you to grow sustainably. These are steps every entrepreneur needs to take, but they're especially crucial in the early stages when your decisions can shape the entire trajectory of your business.

As your business moves into its next phase, you might feel that you've found your footing, but you're ready to scale and grow. This stage can be tricky because the decisions you make here will determine whether your business thrives or plateaus. You may already have a steady stream of income, a small team, and a client base that's growing. But now, you're facing the challenge of scaling up without sacrificing the quality of your services or burning yourself out.

We'll talk about financial planning, team-building strategies, and systems that allow for growth. We'll talk about how to streamline operations, automate certain processes, and ensure you're using your financial resources wisely to fuel expansion.

For those of you further along in your journey, you may already have a fully established business that's profitable and running smoothly. You've mastered the art of delegation, built a strong team, and set up systems that allow your business to run, even without your constant involvement. But what's next? At this stage, many entrepreneurs start thinking about legacy—how they can build something that lasts beyond them and possibly transition their business for sale or succession. I'll share insights into wealth management, long-term business strategies, and even succession planning. This part of the book focuses on leveraging your business as a tool to build generational wealth and ensuring that when you eventually step away from it, your business continues to thrive.

By addressing these different levels, my goal is to empower and equip you with the knowledge and tools to succeed. Entrepreneurs often evolve through these phases, and your needs will change. But having a solid understanding of where you are will help you navigate the challenges and opportunities that come with each level. The journey might look different for each of you, but the goal remains the same: building a business that serves your life and allows you to make an impact.

THE POWER OF CREATING SPACE

I've been an entrepreneur nearly my entire working life. I'm all for working hard, setting intentions for growth, and building businesses that make the world a better place. Like you, I've logged long hours and endured many sleepless nights. I've heard the advice to "slow down" countless times throughout my career, especially as an entrepreneur. But can I be honest with you? Slowing down is not always an option. Entrepreneurs are wired to move fast. When payroll has to be met and your employees and their families depend on you, slowing down doesn't feel like an option.

What I've found to be far more effective is *creating space*—space for creativity, space for listening, space for refueling. This might mean stepping away for a few minutes to breathe, going on a walk, or taking a retreat to clear your mind. It's about carving out moments to be present and reflect—without losing your forward momentum. By doing this, you're not just making time for rest; you're allowing yourself to return to your work more focused, energized, and aligned with your purpose.

I'll share a bit more about this in chapter 10, but Costa Rica has become a place for me to retreat, to find clarity, and to reconnect with myself and God. During one painful season of my life, I was there on a private beach, walking up and down, feeling like I was at the edge of myself. During these walks, I played a song over and over called "Oceans" by Hillsong United. The lyrics spoke to my soul: "Spirit lead me where my trust is without borders / Let me walk upon the waters / Wherever you would call me."[1] I realized that trust was what I needed more than anything—to trust that I was not walking this journey alone and that there was a purpose for all the pain, all the confusion.

The most powerful moment came when I walked back up the mountainside. As I climbed, I saw two white stallions appear, one on either side of me. It felt like a divine message: *I go before you; I stand beside you.* It was a reminder that I wasn't alone, even in the moments when I felt lost and afraid. Later that night, fear crept back in. I heard footsteps outside my room and thought someone was coming to harm me. Grabbing a kitchen knife, I pulled back the curtains, ready to defend myself. But when I looked outside, there was no attacker—just one of those majestic white stallions standing in the moonlight, as if to say, *I'm still here. I still stand with you.*

Sometimes, the message has to be repeated before it sinks in. But once it does, it changes everything. Fear doesn't disappear overnight, and trust isn't a onetime decision—it's a daily practice. I'm positive there have been times you've been afraid you won't have enough money or won't be able to provide for yourself or loved ones. But the real change happens when we take control of our relationship, both with money and with ourselves.

Whenever I face my own hang-ups about money or myself, I try to ask myself, *What would love do in this situation?* Over the years I've learned that love would tell me to let go of the fear, to trust that I am enough, and to use my money not as a measure of my worth but as a tool to live out my purpose. This didn't happen overnight, so I'd like to share my "secret weapon" to how I changed my relationship with money—and myself. It's a vital practice: "I Am's."

THE POWER OF "I AM'S"

"I Am's" are simple declarative affirmations about who you are and who you want to become. When spoken consistently and with intention, they have the power to shift your mindset, unlock your potential, and align your actions with your goals. How we talk to ourselves shapes everything—our decisions, our beliefs, and ultimately our destiny. The words we use to describe ourselves become the truths we live by.

Neuroscientists have found that our thoughts create neural pathways that influence our behaviors and habits. When we consistently speak positive affirmations, we start to rewire our brains for success, empowerment, and growth.[2]

Begin by thinking deeply about who you want to become, then write out your "I Am" statements. Speak them aloud every day. This is not a onetime exercise. It's a daily discipline, a ritual that will shift your mindset, transform your relationship with money, and ultimately shape the course of your life.

Let's get started with the power of "I Am's."

1. **Think About These Things:** Who do you want to become? What do you want to be said about you? What do you stand for? The key here is not to focus on who you currently are or what your life looks like right now, but who you know deep down you were meant to be.

    Every transformation starts with a vision of what's possible. Take a moment to get still and ask yourself these questions: *Who is the most powerful, aligned, and abundant version of me? What does that person look like, act like, and believe?* This vision will guide the affirmations you create.

2. **Write It Out:** We create everything twice—once in our minds and then in the physical world. I like to think of my pen as a magic wand. Every word

written is a step toward becoming that person you envisioned. You don't need to be a wordsmith here; just get started writing things out. For example, your "I Am's" might look like this:

- I am powerful.
- I am kind.
- I am generous.
- I am worthy of success.
- I am capable of achieving my dreams.
- I am loved.
- I am forgiven.
- I am abundant in every area of my life.

The act of writing these down is a way to crystallize your intentions. You're creating a road map for the person you want to become, and each statement acts as a milestone on that journey.

3. **Speak It Out:** This is where the real magic happens. You must speak these "I Am" statements out loud, consistently, until they become a part of you. There's a reason why the phrase "I Am" is so powerful: it's a direct statement of identity. We must shut down the negative stories we've been telling ourselves for years. Every time you catch yourself with a negative thought or statement—*I'm not good enough, I'm not smart enough, I'll never succeed*—replace it with a positive "I Am" statement.

When you say things like, "Money doesn't come easy" or "I'm always struggling," you're speaking that reality into existence. But when you shift to positive, empowering affirmations—"I am financially abundant" or "I am worthy of wealth"—you start to change the script.

4. **The 61-Day Challenge:** For the next sixty-one days, speak out twenty-five new "I Am's" every morning. Repeat them with feeling, believing that each statement is a step toward becoming the person you want to be. If you catch yourself saying something negative during the day, counteract it by immediately declaring ten positive "I Am" statements to retrain your brain and shift your mindset.

If you don't take control of fully stepping into the person you can be, no one will. Friend, you are powerful. You are worthy. You are more than enough. And if you're ever stuck on writing an "I Am" statement, memorize this one and say it to yourself every day: "I am more than enough and never too much."

I can't wait to start this journey with you so that we can set you on a course to live life rich!

When the Vision Is Clear, the Decisions Are Easy

There's a good chance that you're one of my favorite kinds of people. How do I know? Since you're reading this book, you likely either own a business or are looking to start one. That means you're an entrepreneur, or at least on your way. I *love* entrepreneurs.

During my decades as a financial strategist, I've met entrepreneurs from all walks of life and every industry imaginable. We're a crazy bunch! But we're also smart, resilient, resourceful, and won't take no for an answer. We put in the work to grow more than our businesses; we put in the work to grow ourselves. I've rarely met people who were more into personal growth and development than entrepreneurs, because at the end of the day we know we are responsible for the results of our business. We're the generators that power the engine of the economy. We give people jobs, help them provide for their families, fix problems, and spark ideas that move humanity forward.

Entrepreneurs are a rare breed.

Entrepreneurs are the hope of the world.

For that reason, I truly believe that *the world needs you rich*.

Yet for far too many of us, success comes at the expense of our own sanity. We're overextended, burned out, and often the worst boss we've ever had. Seriously, when was the last time you gave yourself a few weeks off? Recently I looked up the definition of *entrepreneur* because it gets thrown around so easily these days. The Oxford dictionary defines it as "a person who organizes and operates a business or businesses, taking on greater than normal financial risks in order to do so."[3]

Greater than normal financial risks.

That describes nearly every entrepreneur I've met, to a T.

When it comes to money, it can feel as if we're lining everyone else's pockets except our own. We carry all the risk, suffer countless sleepless nights, and wonder if we're trapped in a prison of our own making. This isn't the vision most of us had when we launched our business.

So what do we do when the going gets tough?

What any good entrepreneur does, of course! We grind, sell, and hustle. We make things happen because if we don't, no one else will. But you already know how this story ends because you've lived it many times. More sales, longer hours, or the latest productivity hacks won't cut it. Neither will a bigger house, a new spouse, or dropping exorbitant amounts of cash on a collection of sparkly shoes. I've done at least two out of those three (none of your business which ones), so I won't be throwing rocks at anyone. No judgment here!

Speaking of rocks, I'm not sure if you've ever heard of rock picking, but it was a big part of my life growing up. When you're one of eight kids on a North Dakota farm, the powers that be will find anything to keep you busy to keep the farm running. If you're not familiar with rock picking, it refers to literally picking rocks out of a field so that large machines called cultivators can chew through the winter-hardened soil to prepare it for seeding. As you might imagine, it's not a good idea to have rocks hidden in the soil while twelve-inch blades chomp through it.

While my farm days are long past, I still spend a good deal of time rock picking, just now with entrepreneurs. I help people like you identify the hidden things that can break the machine that is your business. Just like on the farm, if the machine breaks, you may not have any food for the coming season.

Rock picking may sound boring and tedious (it is), but you should know this about farmers: the best ones plan everything. Planting and harvesting schedules, equipment maintenance, seed varieties, water usage—*everything*. Planning is a must because any number of things can go wrong: pests, rotting soil, "acts of God," supply chains shutting down—the list goes on and on.

Farm life and business life aren't so different. The difference is that unlike farmers, many entrepreneurs don't have a plan and often just shoot from the hip. If that's you, you may have been able to get to this point without much trouble. Thing is, you can go only so far making things up as you go along.

You need a plan, so where do we start? Throughout the coming chapters I'm going to provide you with a ton of worksheets, diagrams, checklists, and scripts that you're encouraged to work through. You can download them for free at liveliferichbook.com.

Don't just read this book, *do* the book.

I also encourage you to keep a journal. The word *journal* originally meant a written record of the experiences on a journey. A well-kept journal can be a vital part of your growth and can redirect you toward your goals when you go off course. One of my favorite things to do is to go through some of my older journals because they really show how far I've come. Trust me, documenting your journey is one of the best gifts you can give your future self.

TELL ME WHAT YOU REALLY WANT

When meeting with first-time clients I often quote the famous line from the Spice Girls song: "So tell me what

WHEN THE VISION IS CLEAR, THE DECISIONS ARE EASY

you want, what you really, really want."[4] If the song gets stuck in your head now, it might not be a bad thing because being honest about what you want is the first step to getting where you want to go. The age-old quote often attributed to Lewis Carroll still rings true: "If you don't know where you are going, any road will get you there."

Before you tell me that you just want to retire and sit on a beach all day, let's be straight with each other: you're not going to want to do that for longer than a few days. If you ask those who have retired to beach life, most of them will tell you it's not all it's cracked up to be. For goodness' sake, you're an entrepreneur! You probably had ten ideas this past week that could all make a million dollars that you want done by yesterday. Many of my clients who have more than enough money to retire (some for several lifetimes) are really looking for their second or third acts in life, they just don't know it yet. More than beach time, they want significance, fulfillment, and meaning. The good news is, you don't have to wait until retirement for those things. You can experience them now, while on the journey.

So what do you really want? Right now, it might simply be "to be debt free," "to have a million dollars stacked in my nest egg," or "to find the perfect assistant." Let's go a bit deeper than that, shall we? Because if you dig beyond the answers to those questions, you'll often find what you're really looking for. You've got to be clear on what you want. Why?

When the vision is clear, the decisions are easy.

People spend far too much time and effort trying to make the right decisions (especially around money) instead of aligning themselves with the vision they have for life. It's time to reclaim that vision.

Let's start with this simple exercise. This might seem a bit random, especially for a book about money, but stick with me.

You spend so many of your days running around like your hair is on fire. It's time to revisit some of your best days and point your life toward having more of those best days. Think back to three of the best days of your life. Then jot the answers to these questions for each of those days:

1. Where were you?
2. Who was with you, if anyone?
3. What were you doing?
4. How did you feel?
5. Why did you feel this way?
6. Do you want more of this kind of day?
7. What can you do to have more of these kinds of days?

With these days in mind, take some time to think about the vision you have for your ideal business and life. You might be surprised at what you find.

My profession has allowed me to meet some very wealthy people, but it isn't their money that impresses me, it's their mindset. Most of them come from very humble beginnings. They will all tell you that money can be replenished after being lost. Time cannot. The mindset is that every single day is either moving you toward your goal or away from it. Here's one challenge I want to lay before you right off the bat: *never waste a day*.

NEVER WASTE A DAY

To never waste a day doesn't mean that every day is going to be one of your best. Some days are just a grind. I'm not one of those "wake up at 4:00 a.m., jump into a thirty-degree-Fahrenheit cold plunge, crush a two-hour workout, and chug a breakfast shake" people. I love my sleep and could definitely make healthier choices than knoephla for breakfast (it's a North Dakota "cheese button" dish). But when my feet hit the floor every morning as I roll out of bed I say, "I get to choose this day!" If you have a plan, that means every single day can move you closer to what you really want. Even the hardest of days can still be one day closer to what you want.

Never wasting a day is one of my hardest lessons learned. In 2013, I went through a divorce and spent my days "recuperating" by hiding in bed and binging trashy

TV shows. One night my sister Mellie scolded me, saying, "Marissa, it's nine o'clock on a Friday night. You're sad, lonely, and depressed. Get dressed; we're going out."

Mellie is the outgoing one in our family, the kind of person who lights up any room she walks into. She dragged me to an old country bar, the kind that has creaky floors and smells like dollar beers and regret. As she hit the dance floor, a flock of guys immediately rushed around her. To be honest I was a bit annoyed, not at Mellie but more so because I felt like damaged goods. Divorce can do that to you.

Mellie kept doing her thing so I decided to head to the corner booth to wallow. (I swear, I'm way more fun to be around nowadays.) While walking across the bar, some dude asked me to dance. I'm pretty sure I did the "talk to the hand" thing and turned him down without even batting an eye. Five minutes later he came to my seat and asked me to dance again. This time I actually looked at him and, uh, *dayum*. This dude was built like a rock, six foot three, sparkling blue eyes. I didn't know Thor lived in North Dakota.

Still, I turned him down. I just was not in the mood to meet anyone and wanted to get back to my Netflix and ice cream. A few minutes later Thor asked me *yet again*, and just as I was about to tell him off, Mellie locked eyes with me from across the bar, stormed over, and shoved me onto the dance floor with Thor. Thor's real name was James, a former Army sniper who loved monster cars, big trucks, and Miller light beer. This man could dance up a storm and he taught me how to two-step that night.

We danced, laughed, and loved our way through the next few years. He was the kind of guy who texts you every morning saying stuff like, "Good morning, baby. Be the kind of woman that when your feet hit the floor in the morning, all hell shakes and says, 'Oh crap—she's awake!'"

James wasn't just any guy—he was someone who, from the very beginning, made me feel seen and cherished in a way I hadn't experienced before. He had this quiet strength about him, like something out of an old Western movie, where the hero didn't say much but when he did, his words carried weight. He was strong, steady, and fiercely protective, but beyond that, he had a tender, thoughtful side that took me by surprise.

For one hundred days, James sent me a love poem every single morning. Can you imagine that? Every day, without fail, he'd find a poem online that expressed how he felt about me and text it to me. I still have them, tucked away in a file on my phone and iPad. Those poems were his way of telling me I was always on his mind, even when we weren't together. And it wasn't just the poems—he also sent me songs that made him think of me. Country songs, mostly, because that's what he loved, but each one felt like a window into his soul.

One of the most touching things James did happened early in our relationship. I had never gotten my nails done before, but James researched the best nail salons and took me to get my first manicure. He didn't just drop me off—he sat next to me, pulling up a chair beside the nail technician like he was overseeing a delicate operation. He wanted to make sure everything was perfect, that I was happy with the experience. About a quarter of the way through, he even leaned in and told the technician, "She needs to be really happy when this is done."

It was sweet and a little funny because the poor guy doing my nails was a bit scared! When James stepped out to take a call, the technician whispered to me, "Is that man your husband?"

I laughed and said, "No, he's my boyfriend."

The technician looked at me with wide eyes and joked, "He's very scary. I think he might kill me if you're not happy!"

Of course, James wasn't going to hurt anyone; it was just his way of ensuring I had a great experience.

There was also the way he connected with my family. My mom adored him, and he would bring her mint Dilly Bars from Dairy Queen because he knew they were her favorite. It wasn't roses or grand gestures, but the simplicity and thoughtfulness of those Dilly Bars meant everything to her. To this day, she can't eat one without thinking of him. These moments, these acts of love and care, were what made James so special to me.

James was strong, loving, patient, and clearly persistent. When he eventually proposed I was flattered but declined because I was scared to get married again.

James took my rejection like water off a duck's back. He said, "No matter what, you're my forever girl. Just wear this in honor of my grandmother; it's her ring. One day, you'll say yes. I know it." After confirming we were *not* engaged, I started wearing the ring.

Just a few weeks later, a call came from James that changed my life. He said, "Baby, I can't walk." I rushed over to take him to the ER where the doctors found an eight-inch tumor on his spine, neck, and back. The tumor was pressing on his spinal cord, making him unable to walk. It was such a serious situation that he had to be airlifted to Minneapolis for surgery first thing in the morning.

While heading into surgery the next day, James looked at me and laughed, saying, "Well, you can't be the girl that doesn't marry the guy who has cancer. Now you have to say yes!"

James taught me so much about having a positive attitude in difficult situations. His circumstances defined the scene, but his attitude is what really wrote the story. We made a deal that if he walked out of the hospital on his own one day, I'd marry him.

But the road ahead was brutal.

For three months I slept on the chair in James's hospital room. Every single day he'd say something like, "It's a beautiful day in the neighborhood, babe. What's on the rehab agenda today? What do we need to do so we can walk out of here and marry each other?"

The cancer was stage 4 and the chemo was awful, but somehow James's attitude would outshine his circumstances. The medical staff said they'd never seen anyone like him.

Unfortunately, James continued to deteriorate and I took him into home care a few days before Christmas. On Christmas Day, I was praying and pleading to God for a miracle. James lifted my face in his hand, wiped away my tears, and said, "Babe, you've been praying for a miracle, but I already got my miracle the day that I found you. I found my faith, I have a family who loves me, and I know where I'm going, so I need you to make me a promise."

"Of course," I said. "Anything."

He said, "There's something in you, and the world needs you. I need you to make me a promise that you won't spend the next five years living in the bottle or in bed crying. I need you to get up every single day and live. Really live. Never waste a day."

James passed on January 9, 2016, but what he said to me on Christmas Day was one of the greatest gifts I've ever received. *Never waste a day.* I've lived by that principle ever since. Some days are glorious, while others can be heart-wrenching, but they're never wasted. Every day can be a great day or a growth day.

Friend, I know you've had your fair share of hard days. But today, you woke up on the topside of the soil.

You might feel like you're behind, or it's too late, or your circumstances are too overwhelming, but you're still here. Let's make today the day you reclaim the vision you had when you started this crazy journey of entrepreneurship. Let's make today the day you start crafting a plan that makes that vision a reality. Let's choose this day.

We'll get into the money and business talk in the next chapter. But first, tell me what you want, what you really, really want. Better yet, tell yourself what you really, really want. Chew on some of the key takeaways from this chapter, then dive into the questions that follow.

KEY TAKEAWAYS

Let's reflect. Spend time thinking about and taking hold of some of the key points in this chapter:

- The world needs you rich.
- Success can often come at the expense of your own sanity, but it doesn't have to be this way.
- When the vision is clear, the decisions are easy.
- "If you don't know where you are going, any road will get you there."
- Your circumstances might define the scene, but your attitude writes the story.
- Never waste a day.
- Today is going to be a great day or a growth day.
- Choose this day.

LET'S GO DEEPER

Go to liveliferichbook.com, download the guide, and start working through these exercises. Or simply grab a journal, jot down the date, and work through these questions.

1. You're an entrepreneur and part of a rare breed. In what ways have you grown and developed yourself over the years?
2. Success can often come at the expense of your own sanity. Have you ever felt this way? If so, in what ways?
3. What do you really want? What's the vision you have for your business and life?
4. If you haven't done so already, think through three of your best days and jot down the answers to these questions for each day:
   - Where were you?
   - Who was with you, if anyone?
   - What were you doing?
   - How did you feel?
   - Why did you feel this way?
   - Do you want more of this kind of day?
   - What can you do to have more of these kinds of days?

2

Prepare or Repair: Your Freedom Plan

There's a running joke among my kids that I'm just one conspiracy theory away from becoming a full-fledged doomsday prepper. "Preppers" are folks who prepare for society's collapse by stockpiling tons of food, water, and sometimes lots of guns. Some even buy swaths of land so they have a place to live "off the grid" on a moment's notice.

If you're one of these folks, all the power to you. I'm nowhere near being that committed to the prepper life, but if you ever come to my house and look at my pantry, you'll see why my kids joke about me: there's about six months' worth of nonperishable food hoarded in there.

A big reason why I might be like this is because I grew up in a trailer along with my seven siblings. I'm not quite sure how old I was, but one day it really sunk in: we were poor. Not just kinda poor, like kids who complain about not having an iPhone. We were "living in a trailer suffering through winter with a stove for a heater" kind of poor.

One day I said to my mom, "Mom, we're poor, aren't we? Not just poor, but *really, really poor*."

Now, my mom is extremely talkative. She will talk your ear off, anytime, anywhere. This was one of the few encounters with her when she said very little, which is why it stuck.

She replied, "Marissa, will you be a victim or will you be victorious? It's your choice."

That day, I started to learn about the power of perspective. Even if a situation sucks, we often have more choices than we think. But the key is to do our best not to let ourselves get into sucky situations in the first place.

There's a saying I use often these days that I learned from my grandpa while working on the farm: *prepare or repair*. In the last chapter I told you that the best farmers plan everything. In North Dakota, the winters are brutal and the growing seasons are short, so we had to "make hay while the sun is still shining," as Grandpa used to say. It's no different when it comes to your business and life. Prepare or repair. Let's get prepping, shall we?

PREPARE OR REPAIR: YOUR FREEDOM PLAN

PLAN FOR THE LIFE YOU DREAM OF, NOT THE LIFE YOU FEAR

In one of the most famous scenes in film history, Mel Gibson, playing William Wallace in *Braveheart*, cries out, "Freedom!" during his intense final moments.[5] Freedom is so important that many people give up everything for it, and sometimes it takes everything to really get it. Freedom is incredibly important to me, which is why I named one of my first companies thirty years ago after the very concept.

Earlier I asked you to jot down what you really want because when the vision is clear, the decisions become easy. Knowing what you want is part of the overall plan for your business to actualize the life you want. I call this the Freedom Plan. It's a simple plan based on answering these questions:

1. What do you really want?
2. How will you know you've attained it?
3. Who do you want to take with you?
4. Who can help you?
5. Who will get all of it when you're gone?

Working through simple questions like these will give you more clarity. The catch? Just because something is simple doesn't mean it's easy. How many times have you been to the doctor and their advice was to eat better, sleep more, and exercise? Simple, but not easy. Launching a rocket into outer space is a simple concept: create enough energy in a rocket to power it past the pull of gravity into outer space. But you'll never convince me that rocket science is easy.

Money is the same way.

The premise is simple: make money and save more than you spend. But this isn't always easy because we all have our own narratives, behavior, and psychology around money. Some of us have constructed the belief that we'll never get ahead. We have stories around money because of our childhood, which might be why I still hoard six months of food in my pantry.

We'll dig into some numbers shortly, but first let's address something big: the weight of the self-judgment and shame we often face around money. Money, for many, isn't just currency. It's a reflection of our life choices, our values, and sometimes even our self-worth. This emotional tie can keep us from facing our financial realities. Whatever your past may be, let's make this a judgment-free zone.

The first person you have to stop judging is yourself. No one can make you feel inferior without your consent, including you. Your financial history is not your destiny. I totally understand fearing the stories the numbers might reveal, but burying our heads in the sand won't change the narrative. Dwelling on past financial choices won't change them either. No one makes good decisions all the time. Stop beating yourself up. You might as well be nice to yourself; it's who you'll have to spend the rest of your life with!

THE FIRST STEP: GET ORGANIZED

One of the most important steps you can take toward freedom is to get organized. Below you'll find a quick Document Checklist. Gather the items on this list in one place. If you do this now, it will make everything we cover later much easier. You can also download this for free in the workbook at liveliferichbook.com so you can print it out.

Personal Files:

- Tax returns: two years for both business and personal returns
- Balance sheets
- Loan documents
- Wills (health-care directive, power of attorney)
- Trust agreements
- Major asset purchase details

Employer:

- Retirement savings plan statements
- Pension statements
- Payroll or other income statements
- Employee benefits booklets or links

Bank or Credit Union:

- Checking account statements
- Savings / CDs / Money market account statements
- Credit card statements
- Other miscellaneous forms

Investments:

- Investment account statements
- Annuity statements

Insurance Company:

- Life insurance statements
- Long-term care insurance statements
- Health insurance, hospital, major medical policy statements
- Disability income insurance policy information
- Property and casualty policy information

Business:

- Buy-sell agreements
- Deferred compensation agreements
- Stock / options / bonus plans
- Business operating agreement
- Articles of incorporation
- State filing forms

- P&L statement
- Balance sheet

You may not be able to gather all the items in one shot, but gather them sooner rather than later. There is never a convenient time for life to throw you a curveball.

Now, let's talk about your Freedom Plan.

THE FREEDOM PLAN

Let's take our planning a bit further. Grab a journal and write these numbers down:

1. **Determine your Freedom Number:** This is the amount of money you need to maintain your lifestyle *for the rest of your life*. I prefer to make this an annual number because it's easier to work backward from there. How much do you need every month or year to live your dream life?

2. **Identify your Freedom Sources:** This is all about spotting your moneymakers. What are you already earning income from? This could be things like rent from a property, a pension, profits from your business, royalties, and so on. Jot these down along with the approximate amount of money from each source, monthly or annually.

3. **Set your Freedom Date:** Your freedom date is the date in which you no longer have to go to work for anyone anytime in the future, including

yourself. Set a realistic date, based on your Freedom Number and Freedom Sources, where this is potentially possible.

Freedom Number

Your Freedom Number is the linchpin of your financial plan. Let's say you need $10,000 every month to live comfortably. Let's multiply that by 12 to get the annual number: $120,000 ($10,000 × 12 = $120,000). Obviously this number doesn't account for inflation or taxes, so let's bump this up a bit. To truly have $120,000 at your disposal each year, you might need to target an annual figure closer to $150,000. This is the yearly sum that will pave the way for your dream life. If you want more later, you can always increase it. I may have grown up a farm girl but now I'm a fan of sparkly shoes, so I've upped my Freedom Number over the years.

Freedom Sources

The next step is identifying where this money will come from: your Freedom Sources. No plan should have a single point of failure, so having multiple income streams is vital. Consider the possibility of a modest pension. Or perhaps you're receiving Social Security. You might also have a 401(k), a rental property, or even an agricultural venture bringing in money.

Next, make your money your best employee. In other words, we want your money making more money. Think about how you can position your profits and invest to generate income, and utilize the suggestions below for inspiration on how to do so:

1. Put money back into your own business for growth.
2. Invest in other people's businesses (stocks, bonds, etc.).
3. Invest in real estate.

This approach is called *the bucket strategy*, and we'll delve deeper into it in chapter 5. One path forward is to fill the first two buckets and then set aside a remaining percentage for real estate. Obviously that comes with risk, and one of the most common pitfalls has to do with running out of cash flow or not having enough cash on hand.

Many real estate owners are just one extended vacancy away from real trouble. If you own a rental property, jot down the money that comes in but make sure to subtract:

- Taxes on the property
- Insurance on the property
- Maintenance on the property

If you have equity in a business, that can hold substantial value. If you're still running your business, you'll need to think about whether you'll eventually sell that business outright or build a team that runs it so you can receive a cut of the profits later through a K-1 distribution. (A K-1 distribution is essentially a payout you receive from a business partnership you're in. Suppose a partnership earned $100,000 in net income during the year, and you own 25 percent of the partnership. Your K-1 would report $25,000 as your share of the partnership's income, which you would then include on your personal tax return and be responsible for paying taxes on.)

Freedom Date

Next, let's set your Freedom Date. By marking a Freedom Date, you're not just setting a deadline; you're challenging yourself to be intentional with the time you have. Time will pass no matter what. Days turn into months, and months into years. Time can be your ally if you use it wisely, consistently, and with a clear vision of the day you reach your Freedom Number. Never waste a day.

You'd be surprised how few entrepreneurs actually know their Freedom Number, Freedom Sources, and Freedom Date. If the thought of just working through these exercises makes you uncomfortable, that's a good clue that you should keep pressing in. This exercise will take you just about ten minutes. Those ten minutes will pass whether you work through them or not, but if you face the resistance and work through your Freedom Number, Freedom Sources, and Freedom Date, you'll take a huge step forward into actualizing the life you really want.

I'm pushing you hard on this because I've seen way too many instances where entrepreneurs are caught off guard because of something out of their control—be it sickness, a market crash, a bad hire, or anything else. Borrow a bit of my prepper mentality and start planning by working through these numbers. Prepare or repair, the choice is yours.

THE THREE BUSINESS PHASES

All this talk about freedom might feel a bit premature, but I'm a big believer in the concept of beginning with the end in mind. Let's take a big-picture look at the different stages of development that your business will need to go through to bring the Freedom Plan to life.

Phase 1: Big Challenges & Big Opportunities

In the initial phase, you're laying the groundwork for your business. The focus here is on setting clear goals and establishing a solid structure to support your vision.

- **Goals:** It's essential to start with a clear vision of where you want your business to go. Setting specific, long-term goals will guide your decisions and strategies.
- **Business Structure:** Choosing the right legal and organizational structure is critical for tax purposes, liability, and growth potential.
- **Pitfalls & Predators—Structured Agreements:** Be aware of common pitfalls and set up structured agreements to protect your business interests.
- **The Big 5:** Identify and prioritize the five most crucial areas or tasks that will drive your business forward.
- **Building a Team:** Assemble a team that shares your vision and can help you achieve your goals.
- **Questions to Consider:** Continually ask yourself key questions to ensure you're on the right track and prepared for future challenges.

Phase 2: Protection & Prosperity

As your business grows, so does the complexity and the need for protection and strategic management of resources.

- **Predators—Taxes & Inflation:** Protect your business from the financial predators of taxes and inflation by planning and strategizing accordingly.
- **Pitfalls—Protection from the Unknown:** Guard against unexpected events and risks by having robust protection measures in place.
- **Positioning Profits—3 Buckets:** Organize your profits into three categories (short-term, intermediate, and legacy) to ensure balanced and sustainable growth.
- **Key Players—Difference Makers:** Identify and leverage key players who can significantly impact your business's success.
- **Questions to Consider:** Reevaluate and refine your strategies based on critical questions to maintain and enhance prosperity.

Phase 3: Achieving Freedom

The final phase focuses on ensuring that your business can operate independently and that you achieve the freedom you desire.

- **Exit Strategies & Succession:** Plan for the future by developing exit strategies and succession plans to ensure your business's longevity.
- **Business Valuation—Know Your Worth:** Regularly evaluate your business to understand its market value and make informed decisions.
- **Built to Sell or Built for Legacy?** Decide whether your business is being built to sell for a profit or to be passed on as a legacy.
- **Legacy Planning:** Plan how your business will contribute to your legacy and impact future generations.
- **Questions to Consider:** Continually ask pivotal questions to guide your decision-making and strategic planning.
- **What's Next?** Always be ready to consider the next steps and opportunities for growth and expansion.

By understanding and addressing the unique needs and priorities of each phase, you can ensure that your business not only survives but thrives, ultimately leading to the financial freedom and fulfillment you've envisioned.

DESTINATION: FREEDOM

In the previous chapter you took time to think through three of your best days. Now it's time to think about the best days still to come. Vision empowers you; it's part of preparing for the life you want. Without it you can't get excited about the future or keep your passion high enough to keep going when faced with obstacles.

One of the most helpful ways to do this is to create a bucket list—a list of things to do before you "kick the bucket." This is a collection of personal goals, experiences, and achievements you want to accomplish. Your bucket list is a passport to a life less ordinary and your Freedom Plan will make this list a reality.

Before you dive into your bucket list, allow me to pose a question that takes all of this to another level: Who are you taking with you? In other words, who are you making the experience of life that much sweeter for? Who will you share your memories with? That infuses your bucket list with a whole new type of energy.

True wealth isn't just about what you have; it's about what you share. In 2019, I traveled through Europe for thirty-five days with my youngest daughter, Danielle. We dubbed it our "Freedom Tour" and it included stops in Greece, London, and Paris. But the highlight of the trip for me was St. Petersburg, Russia.

My grandparents were Ukrainian, so visiting this region connected me to my roots. The city was even more stunning than I imagined. The elaborate architecture, the vibrant culture, the stunning palaces—I felt like I was in a fairy tale. We visited the Winter Palace and I just had to dance on the same floors where kings and queens used to host their galas.

Sure, Danielle had a few "Is my mom really doing that" moments and pretended she didn't know me, but I didn't care. It was pure magic! My "dream come true" moment was watching *Swan Lake* by Tchaikovsky at the Mariinsky Theatre. I'd dreamed of going to *Swan Lake* my entire life, and there was no better place to do it than at the first place it was performed, right in St. Petersburg. Danielle and I forged memories that nourish our souls to this day. Doing this was on my bucket list, and my Freedom Plan made this possible.

So let's have some fun, shall we? Dreaming about and setting your intentions for freedom should be fun! Grab your journal and write down your answers to whatever questions jump out at you from this list:

1. What three cities or countries do you want to visit?
2. Are there historical or natural wonders you dream of seeing in person?
3. What concerts, festivals, shows, or sporting events do you want to attend?
4. What personal or professional goal do you want to accomplish? (Finish a marathon? Write a book?)
5. What cultural dish, food adventure, or fancy restaurant have you had on your list to try?
6. Is there anything that might make you a bit nervous but you're curious to try? (Skydiving?

Performing a lead role in a play? Running with the bulls in Spain?)
7. Is there a charitable act or contribution you want to make, like building a school or volunteering abroad?
8. What's one thing you'd regret not doing when you look back on your life years from now?

How does it feel to cast a vision for your future? To actually allow yourself to be honest with your dreams, wants, and desires? It's not enough to just desire something; it's also necessary to know that you deserve it. Your sense of deserving is usually something that is formed when you're very young. Even now, you may be holding on to conclusions you made about what you should get and why. This was certainly the case for me. The good news is that you still hold the pen in your hand and can rewrite how your story goes.

KEY TAKEAWAYS

Let's reflect. Spend time thinking about and taking hold of some of the key points in this chapter:

- Prepare or repair. The choice is yours.
- Plan for the life you dream of, not the life you fear.
- The first person you have to stop judging is yourself.

- No one can make you feel inferior without your consent, including you.
- Your bucket list is a passport to a life less ordinary.
- True wealth isn't just about what you have; it's about what you share.

LET'S GO DEEPER

Go to liveliferichbook.com, download and print the guide, and start working through these exercises. Or simply grab a journal, jot down the date, and work through these questions.

1. Write down your Freedom Number.
2. Write down your Freedom Sources.
3. Write down your Freedom Date.
4. If you haven't already, think over these bucket-list questions and write responses to any that jump out at you:
   - What three cities or countries do you want to visit?
   - Are there historical or natural wonders you dream of seeing in person?
   - What concerts, festivals, shows, or sporting events do you want to attend?
   - What personal or professional goal do you want to accomplish?

- What cultural dish, food adventure, or fancy restaurant have you had on your list to try?
- Is there anything that might make you a bit nervous but you're curious to try?
- Is there a charitable act or contribution you want to make?
- What's one thing you'd regret not doing when you look back on your life years from now?

Assemble Your Freedom Team

One of my favorite things about being an entrepreneur is that business can take you to cool places and provide you with rich experiences. Some time ago I found myself in a small village called Lisdoonvarna, along the rugged west coast of Ireland. My host was Joanne Hession, a business powerhouse who has trained over eighty thousand entrepreneurs on how to do business better, smarter, and more successfully through her company, Entrepreneurs Academy (entrepreneursacademy.ie).

I was in Ireland to speak at an event and Joanne arranged a trip to a renowned salmon smokehouse called the Burren Smokehouse. Waves crashing against the cliffs, the aroma of salty sea air mixed with smoking wood—now this was living! The genius behind this culinary haven is a lady named Birgitta, and she's not just your average chef. As a young child, Birgitta would accompany her father to the local smokehouse in her native Sweden to smoke the eel that they caught together. These childhood memories of smoking fish inspired her and her husband, Peter, to open their very own spot. Birgitta has served her prized salmon to the queen of England and other global dignitaries. People travel thousands of miles just to experience the magic she crafts in her smokehouse.

Call me weird, but when I see a successful operation, I see much more than just the visionary or owner. I see all the people, processes, and moving parts necessary to make it happen. (You should see me when I walk through Disney World; it's impossible for me not to think about how much happens behind the scenes to make it all work.)

IT STARTS WITH YOU, BUT IT GROWS WITH MANY

Whether it's Birgitta's salmon smokehouse, Disney World, or a local small business, true success always requires a team.

Growing up, I often heard, "If it's gonna be, it's up to me." That mantra echoed in my head for years. There are many who have adopted this mindset, not out of choice but out of necessity. If enough time passes, the idea of rugged individualism becomes familiar and even comforting. Sometimes it can feel like you're the only one you can trust or rely on. I get it.

But let's pump the brakes, fellow Lone Ranger. Embracing collaboration and receiving help doesn't diminish you; it sets you on the path to true success.

It starts with you, but it grows with many.

It starts with "me" and ends with "we."

Henry Ford once said, "You can take my factories, burn up my buildings, but give me my people and I'll build the business right back again." Great business owners know that people are what drive the business forward or bring it to its demise.

One of the surprising reasons building a team helps you get things done is that a team forces you to focus. You have a team that's standing at the ready asking you, "Why are we doing this? What's our next move?" Essentially, the team needs to understand the dream.

If you're anything like me, you have a hundred new ideas a week and you want them all done yesterday. Oh, how I've wished for a magic wand that would make all my ideas come to life. But the reality is that most entrepreneurs are "idea rich and execution poor." Every choice you make is either pulling you off course or propelling you toward your true north. When presented with new opportunities, get in the habit of asking yourself: *Direction or distraction?*

DEVELOP YOUR FREEDOM TEAM

Let's take a look at key players you need to have on your Freedom Team. They will help you build and execute your Freedom Plan. Many hands make light work.

There are a few layers to my Freedom Team and I'm going to break this down first by two broad categories: personal and professional. We will look at personal team members first, then we'll take a deeper look at your professional team. Let's start with your personal team.

PERSONAL FREEDOM TEAM

The members of your personal team include your:

1. Partner/Spouse
2. Children
3. Extended family
4. Friends
5. Community

Understanding your personal team is crucial because these are the people who provide support, encouragement, and guidance in your life. Your partner or spouse is often your closest confidant and shares in your joys and struggles. They provide emotional support and help you navigate life's challenges.

Your children play a significant role in shaping your priorities and values, and their well-being is likely a driving force behind your decisions.

Extended family members, friends, and community also contribute to your personal support network. Whether it's lending a listening ear, offering practical assistance, or simply being there in times of need, these individuals form the fabric of your personal team. They provide diverse perspectives, experiences, and resources that enrich your life and help you navigate its complexities.

Your personal team represents your foundation, the people who stand by you through thick and thin. Understanding their importance and nurturing these relationships can enhance your overall well-being and contribute to your success in both personal and professional realms.

THE BOARD YOU CAN'T AFFORD

When it comes to your professional Freedom Team members, the first group is your personal advisory board. My friend and host in Ireland, Joanne Hession, calls this the "board you can't afford." That is such an appropriate term for this group because if you were to hire all these folks individually, it would cost a fortune.

So why would they help you? Because people flock to those who have a clear vision for life. Success often breeds generosity. Accomplished leaders and minds often look for others to mentor, advise, and pour into. This team can give you fresh perspectives and sometimes the hard truths you might be reluctant to face. They will come with their own connections, networks, and opportunities, so consider various roles and individuals who can provide well-rounded guidance in multiple areas. Here are some practical roles to consider:

1. **The Visionary:** Someone who can help you dream big and see the broader picture. They inspire you to think outside the box and pursue ambitious goals.
2. **The Mentor:** Someone who's been where you want to go and can guide you based on their experiences. They offer wisdom from lessons learned and can help you avoid pitfalls.
3. **The Peer:** A colleague or friend on a similar life or career trajectory as you. They understand your current challenges and can offer relevant advice or act as a sounding board.
4. **The Industry Insider:** If you're in a particular profession or industry, this person is well-connected and knows the ins and outs, current trends, and can offer specialized guidance.
5. **The Contrarian:** An individual who thinks differently and isn't afraid to challenge your ideas. They'll push you to consider all angles and ensure you're not in an echo chamber.
6. **The Emotional Supporter (the 3:00 a.m. friend):** Often a close friend or family member,

this person is there for emotional and moral support, ensuring you maintain mental and emotional well-being. I call them "3:00 a.m. friends" because you can call them at 3:00 a.m.!
7. **The Networker:** A super-connector who knows everyone. They can introduce you to potential collaborators, employers, partners, or others who can assist in your endeavors.
8. **The Health Nut:** Health is wealth, and if you don't have people pushing you in this all-important area, you're neglecting this most important piece of your plan: you. This might be a nutritionist, fitness coach, or functional medicine doctor.
9. **The Accountability Partner:** This individual keeps you on track, ensuring you follow through on your commitments and goals. They're there to push you when needed and to celebrate your successes.

Did any names pop up for you as you went through the list? Jot them down and set an intention to reach out and do what you can to stay connected to them in meaningful ways.

If you need to make a new connection and have a mutual acquaintance, you can use an email like this one:

To: Kevin
From: Marissa
Subject: Introducing me to Davy Jones

Hey Kevin,

I noticed you're connected to Davy Jones at [company]. I would love to chat with him to get some advice about [topic]. I promise to be respectful of his time.

Would you mind connecting me? I can send you a pre-written email to make things easy for you.

Is that OK?

Thanks,
Marissa

Assuming Kevin says yes, I then send this email:

Thanks, Kevin! Here's a pre-written email. Should be good to send but feel free to edit if you'd like:

SUBJECT: Davy, meet Marissa (a friend)—Marissa, meet Davy

Davy, please meet Marissa.

Marissa is a friend of mine and currently [what you do]. She's excellent at [what you do] and curious about some ways you could connect. She is wondering if you could spare ten minutes to chat on the phone.

Marissa, can you take it from here?

Thanks,
Kevin

I use this all the time when connecting folks or looking for connections within my network.

DO, DUMP, OR DELEGATE

Every week I meet entrepreneurs who say they don't have enough time. How you use your time will make or break your success, and this is another reason you need a team. I once heard it said, "If you don't have an assistant, then you are one." Harsh, but true. If you bill clients at $200 an hour, it's counterproductive to do tasks that someone else can do for $20 an hour.

The biggest asset in your life and business is your time. You must free yourself up for higher-level activities that truly tap into your expertise and potential. When tasks come across my desk, I always use this question to guide me: *Is this something I need to do, dump, or delegate?*

Do It:

- What must you do daily to make money in your business?

- Do you make $10 an hour, $50 an hour, $100 an hour, or $1,000+ for whatever task you are working on?

Dump It:

- What are the least effective tasks you do? These are the tasks that steal your ROI, where you aren't working at your real hourly rate.

Delegate It:

- What are the tasks that need to be done but should never be done at your hourly rate?
- Are you thinking "like a boss" when it comes to delegating tasks?

Using this framework can help you understand how to leverage your time and create a laser-focused, impact-filled day.

How to Figure Your Dollars for Hours

Understanding the true value of your time is a fundamental step for any business owner. Here's how to calculate your hourly rate based on different income levels, helping you determine whether certain tasks are worth your time.

The calculation starts with a standard work year:

- Average year: 40 hours per week × 52 weeks = 2,080 hours

Using this, you can see how different hourly rates translate into annual income:

- $10.00/hour × 2,080 hours/year = $20,800/year
- $50.00/hour × 2,080 hours/year = $104,000/year
- $100.00/hour × 2,080 hours/year = $208,000/year
- $250.00/hour × 2,080 hours/year = $520,000/year

Your net income is what truly matters, which is calculated as:

$$\text{Income} - \text{Expenses} = \text{Net income}$$

This straightforward formula highlights the importance of understanding not just how much you earn but how much you keep after covering all expenses.

Is the Task Worthy of Your Time?

By determining your hourly rate, you can assess whether specific tasks are worth your time and energy. If a task doesn't align with your calculated hourly rate, delegate it to someone else. This allows you to focus on high-impact activities that truly drive your business forward. You may not be able to do this right away, but it's something to work toward.

This exercise isn't just about knowing your worth; it's about making informed decisions that maximize your productivity and profitability. By understanding the true value of your time, you can better prioritize tasks and invest in areas that yield the highest returns.

THE POWERHOUSE BEHIND YOUR ENTERPRISE: TAX, LEGAL, RISK, AND WEALTH

What I'll cover here are Freedom Team members who are part of your enterprise overall but outside of your actual day-to-day business. They will help guide you through the many decisions regarding your business and overall life plan.

Back in chapter 1 I told you that I've spent my fair share of time with loved ones in hospitals. When you or someone you care about is heading in for a major procedure, you don't want a jack-of-all-trades in the room, you want the entire Mayo Clinic. By that I mean you want individuals who are exceptionally skilled in surgery, anesthetics, operating complex medical equipment, post-op care, and each individual part of the procedure. We understand this concept intuitively in medicine but often overlook it when it comes to the health of our enterprise.

Having generalists who dabble in a bit of everything won't cut it. You need specialists—people who excel in their fields—to bring your vision to life. These folks occupy the "core four" buckets of tax, legal, risk, and wealth, and to me, they're like the Mayo Clinic of my enterprise:

- **Accountant:** They ensure your books are accurate. By interpreting the data and laying it bare, they uncover opportunities for cost-saving and profit-making. In essence, they turn your ledgers into a strategic road map. If you're doing this on your own right now, ask yourself again whether this is truly something that should get your valuable time.
- **Attorney:** In the fluctuating landscapes of law and ever-evolving regulations, your attorney ensures you are protected, compliant, and safeguarded against potential pitfalls. Depending on what you do, you may need more than one attorney. For example, if you write books or sell courses, you'll need an intellectual property attorney.
- **Banker:** Your banker is the lifeline to your capital needs, offering the financial products and services that keep your business moving. They assist with securing loans, managing cash flow, and providing insights into how best to leverage your financial assets. A strong relationship with a

knowledgeable banker can open doors to opportunities and support your growth ambitions.
- **Coach/Mentor:** A coach or mentor provides the wisdom and perspective that comes only from experience. They guide you through challenges, help you stay focused on your goals, and provide the motivation to keep pushing forward. Their role is to help you see the bigger picture, develop your leadership skills, and avoid common pitfalls.
- **Financial Adviser:** A great financial adviser goes beyond merely crunching numbers. They know your goals and act as a strategist, helping you navigate the complexities of investments and assets. Their expertise helps manage your risk, guides you to grow, and protects your wealth.
- **Investor:** Think of your investor as the headhunter of your financial enterprise, helping you seize opportunities. When a golden chance presents itself, you want this person to let you know.
- **Insurance Adviser:** Your insurance adviser is a shield-bearer, scanning the horizon for potential storms and pitfalls. They craft safeguards to protect you, ensuring that any and all scenarios are covered.

To build a successful relationship with these advisers, it's crucial to communicate your needs and goals clearly.

You have the right to be straightforward about the relationship, aligning it with your current circumstances, short-term goals, and long-term ambitions. Outline their roles, goals, and responsibilities.

Your Freedom Team is a long-term partnership. It should consist of advisers who tailor plans to your unique situation, take the time to understand your goals, and provide honest feedback, even if it's not what you want to hear.

KEY QUESTIONS TO ASK YOUR PROFESSIONAL FREEDOM TEAM

Very few entrepreneurs will take this next step, but those who do skyrocket their results. It can feel like herding cats, but do everything in your power to make this happen. Gather all the members of your "Mayo Clinic" together—your accountant, attorney, financial adviser, loan officer (investor), insurance agent, and so forth. If they can't be in the same physical room, bring them together in a virtual space.

The first meeting will be the most important and it's all about determining a plan for success and growth. Note that if you are the top client of your advisers or you discover they've never worked with someone running a business similar to yours, it's a red flag.

Here's a streamlined list of questions to guide your first, pivotal meeting toward success and growth:

- **Current Financial Health:** "Can we review the current profit and loss statement? Where are the gaps?"
- **Financial Preservation:** "What strategies can we implement to reduce unnecessary losses?"
- **Wealth Management:** "How can we focus on earning more, retaining earnings, and increasing our investments?"
- **Immediate Actions:** "What are the top three priorities I should focus on right now?"
- **Review of Investments:** "Which of my recent investments haven't generated the expected return on investment?"
- **Benchmarking:** "How are my peers optimizing their income and investment strategies?"
- **Leveraging New Opportunities:** "What recent changes or opportunities can we capitalize on?"
- **Strategic Adjustments:** "What restructuring should be considered now and in the upcoming quarter?"
- **Risk Management:** "Considering my recent acquisitions (such as properties or new hires), what steps should I take to mitigate risks effectively?"
- **Insurance Strategies:** "How can we ensure I'm getting the best insurance rates, and what's the optimal insurance coverage ratio for my situation?"
- **Team Coordination:** "Who on my team will take the lead in coordinating these efforts to ensure

we're working cohesively toward my financial goals?"
- **Year-over-Year Analysis:** "Compared to last year, where do I stand in terms of investments and savings?"
- **Maximizing Retirement Contributions:** "Based on the tax code, how much can I contribute to my retirement plans this year to maximize tax advantages?"
- **Comprehensive Financial Planning:** "Can we conduct a thorough review of my entire financial portfolio, including after-tax investments and real estate, considering taxes and inflation?"
- **Assume You/They Are Missing Something:** "What are we missing?"
- **Next Steps:** "What are the immediate next steps I should take following this meeting?"

The key to these meetings is not just to ask questions but to actively engage with the answers, create actionable plans, and follow through with the guidance provided by your advisory team. Even if you can't gather everyone in the same room at the same time, it's crucial to obtain these answers from each individual, pulling together their expertise to guide your decisions.

Whether you meet with them all at once or at different times, run the entire plan by each and ask, "Do you concur or not?"

The only mistake you can make is not asking for help. Demand more from your team. Get them all working in tandem for your benefit. This can make a world of difference, especially during uncertain economic times.

When the world was grappling with the COVID-19 pandemic, my banker was proactive, reaching out with vital information about the Paycheck Protection Program (PPP) and Economic Injury Disaster Loan (EIDL), explaining what financial aid was available for my businesses in Florida and North Dakota. It's this kind of foresight and initiative that makes a world of difference.

Always look for finishers. It doesn't matter if they're contractors or employees; what matters is they get stuff done. Only reward finished work. If it's half-baked, then it's not done. Guide your team on what "game days" look like—those full-throttle, all-in workdays.

If you want these kinds of folks on your team, show them the big picture—help them see and catch the vision of your business. When they understand the impact of their work, they're more likely to follow through.

Embrace teamwork, friend. The beauty of building your empire is found not just in its achievements but in the hands and hearts that help you build it.

KEY TAKEAWAYS

- It starts with you, but it grows with many.
- Many hands make light work.

ASSEMBLE YOUR FREEDOM TEAM

- Direction or a distraction?
- The right team can both collapse and expand time.
- If you don't have an assistant, you are one. (Ouch!)
- Do, dump, or delegate.
- If you are the top client of your advisers or discover they've never worked with someone running a business similar to yours, it's a red flag.

LET'S GO DEEPER

Go to liveliferichbook.com, download and print the guide, and start working through these exercises. Or simply grab a journal, jot down the date, and work through these questions.

Let's start identifying who is on your personal advisory board. Jot their name down next to the role. If you don't have anyone there yet, write down who you think it could be or who you know that can connect you to the right person to fill that spot on the roster.

- **The Visionary:** _____
- **The Mentor:** _____
- **The Peer:** _____
- **The Industry Insider:** _____
- **The Contrarian:** _____
- **The Emotional Supporter (the 3:00 a.m. friend):** _____
- **The Networker:** _____

- The Health Nut: _____
- The Accountability Partner: _____

Now let's look at your team for tax, legal, risk, and wealth. If you don't have anyone there yet, write down who you think it could be or who you know that can connect you to someone who could fill that spot on the roster.

- Accountant: _____
- Attorney: _____
- Banker: _____
- Coach/Mentor: _____
- Financial Adviser: _____
- Investor: _____
- Insurance Adviser: _____

4

The Art of the Introduction

Small business isn't for the faint of heart. According to the US Bureau of Labor Statistics, the numbers show the road ahead won't be easy:

- 20 percent fail in year one
- 30 percent in year two
- 50 percent after five years
- 70 percent after ten years[6]

That means only 30 percent of businesses are still standing after ten years. This isn't meant to scare you but to be real about what it takes to start, run, and grow a successful business. One of the best ways to ensure your success and longevity is to grow your network.

Your business will go through many phases over the years. Your network will be one of the most powerful assets you have through the ups and downs, but it's not just enough to have a network. Your network needs to be a "net that works"—opening new doors, opportunities, and connections.

Unfortunately for many entrepreneurs, they're not quite sure how to grow their network. They're often so busy working in their business that they have very little time left to build their network. Recently an entrepreneur friend of mine, Mike Kim, shared the job description he gave himself. He said he has three jobs:

- cast vision,
- remove friction, and
- build bridges.

I love this perspective. Keep this list on your whiteboard, work station, and even your refrigerator if you have to.

We touched on vision in the first chapter, and in the last chapter we talked about building a team to remove friction. Now we turn our attention to building bridges and the art of the introduction.

KMART TAUGHT ME EVERYTHING ABOUT INTRODUCTIONS

Remember Kmart? For you younger folks, Kmart is the old-school big-box store (you can think of it as a less-upscale version of Target). They're still around and not as popular as they once were, but Kmart holds a special place in my heart because it's where I learned how to introduce myself to others.

Many of these introductions happened in the baby aisle of my local Kmart. When I was just seventeen years old, I got pregnant with my first child and my whole world changed. Back then, at least where I lived, if you got pregnant, you got married. Because I was still a high school student, my only option was to attend an "alternative school," a place for those of us who were different: pregnant students, substance users, and troubled teens.

I felt completely out of place there and was dead set to get out quickly because my baby was due in just two and a half months. I approached my teachers and principal and proposed a seemingly impossible idea: let me complete my entire senior year in that short time. They were concerned it would be too difficult. I replied, "You don't know my strength. Just give me one chance." Eventually they agreed, and once I committed, they stood by me and kept saying, "Marissa, you've got this. You're meant for more than this place."

I hit the books hard, up to eighteen hours a day. It was intense but my effort paid off and I graduated in record time. I still remember holding Lexi when she was born and whispering, "Baby girl, this is our new beginning."

New beginnings can be great, but I also needed to find work because this baby wasn't going to raise herself! In those days, survival was the name of the game and I did whatever I could to get by. I sold Avon cosmetics door-to-door, delivered phone books (remember those?), sold ads for placemats and stadium seats, and even walked around town with a big heavy-duty trash bag picking up aluminum cans and glass bottles to turn in for change at the recycling center.

I used the little money I scratched together to buy diapers and other baby items, but I also took a small portion of that money to invest in myself. I purchased books and tapes by personal development experts like Tony Robbins, Zig Ziglar, Jim Rohn, and John Maxwell. I learned early on that what you feed your mind each day really matters, and this prepared my mindset for bigger things to come.

My aunt Donna gave me my first real opportunity. She worked in insurance and had a box full of index cards with names of people who hadn't been contacted by their insurance agent in ages. She called them "orphan policyholders." My job? Call them up and set appointments for her. Aunt Donna offered me five dollars for every appointment I set. This was huge for me at the time because I was living in a trailer selling whatever I could to make ends meet, even hosting garage sales to scrape together extra cash.

I got busy setting appointments, starting first thing in the morning and going until late at night. I was on a mission, filling up Aunt Donna's schedule so tight she barely had time to catch her breath. But hey, for five dollars an appointment, we were both determined to make it work.

Those five-dollar bills added up, making a real difference in my life. They were the difference between having diapers for my baby or not. Aunt Donna and her colleagues took note of how good I was and suggested I become an insurance agent. Aunt Donna handed me a stack of books to study and get licensed. Time to hit the books, again!

Starting out I had very few contacts, so I struck up conversations with moms in the baby aisle at Kmart while shopping. I'd introduce myself, chat about everyday life, and eventually talk about what I did and how I helped people. I was learning to build bridges in Kmart of all places.

What started as a five-dollar commission has blossomed today into a thriving business. The effort I put into selling insurance paid off and my sales record spoke for itself. I asked Aunt Donna to introduce me to her contacts at a big insurance company. Despite being under twenty-one at the time, my record impressed them enough to give me a shot.

My position was all commission-based with no fancy office or guaranteed pay, but I was up for the challenge. At meetings, I was introduced to several amazing mentors who advised me to take notes, listen to how the pros spoke to their clients, and understand the solutions they offered. Every step along the way I learned how to effectively introduce myself to others and how that would often open doors that weren't opened for others.

When I eventually moved into financial planning, the art of the introduction became even more paramount to my success. It's one thing to know about securities, licenses, taxes, and legal structures. It's a whole different skill set to connect with people from all walks of life about one of the most important, private, and personal things in their lives: their money.

SOFT SKILLS LEAD TO CONCRETE RESULTS

Renowned investor Warren Buffett once said, "In the business world, unfortunately, the rearview mirror is always clearer than the windshield."[7] Looking back, the soft skill of learning to effectively introduce myself and others has been one of the most quietly powerful tools for expanding my business. The investment I made in the aisles of Kmart has paid countless dividends. The art of the introduction is one of those soft skills that doesn't scream for attention yet fuels long-term growth. Every handshake and exchange taught me that business isn't just transactional, it's relational.

The wealthiest people in the world look for and build networks while everyone else just looks for more work. I love what Ivan Misner, entrepreneur and founder of BNI, said: "Networking is more about farming than it is about hunting."[8] In the fast-paced and ever-evolving landscape of entrepreneurship, it's often these intangible abilities that set apart thriving businesses from the rest.

Moreover, in an increasingly digital world where face-to-face interactions are becoming less frequent, mastering soft skills becomes even more necessary. A single introduction can open doors that seemed locked forever.

The art of the introduction also plays a huge part in how you build your team. Imagine you make a new hire. How you introduce your current team to this new hire (and vice versa) can set the tone for how everyone will work together. Say you introduce your new hire to the team and say, "Hey, everyone, meet Trish, she's here to do all the things none of you really want to do. Catch up with her later, if you feel like it." Needless to say, Trish isn't going to be set up for success and your team will look like a bunch of lazy people who don't care about anyone. Soft skills are the glue that binds teams together, fostering collaboration and cultivating a positive work culture.

Let's take a look at how you introduce yourself. The same principles can be adapted when you introduce someone else. When it comes to the art of the introduction, it's important to work through the following five steps:

1. Get clear on who you are and what you do.
2. Identify the Seven Major Headaches you solve.
3. Determine the cost of not hiring (or knowing) you.
4. Help others help you.
5. Craft your perfect pitch.

Generally, these cover two types of introductions. The first is how you introduce yourself and the second is how others introduce you. You have control over the first because you are simply introducing yourself. The second needs to be something you shape with intention. Don't leave this to chance. If you do, you may end up being connected to others in the same way as Trish in my fictional example.

STEP 1: GET CLEAR ON WHO YOU ARE AND WHAT YOU DO

Picture this: You're walking into a room full of new faces or attending a networking event. Have you ever been in that spot where you introduce yourself and then find yourself rambling about what you do? Cue your biggest fear: the other person starts to zone out.

If you've ever felt like you've got so much to say that you don't even know where to begin, you're not alone. The key is to pinpoint who you are, what you do, and how you can be a game-changer for whoever you're talking to.

Let's start at step one: Who are you, exactly? How would you describe yourself? Oftentimes we can get stuck seeing ourselves solely through our professional role. I want you to get a bit more personal with this and think through the whole vibe you're about. Remember in an earlier chapter when I mentioned that my sister Mellie is the life of the party? That's what I'm referring to.

Sometimes, the hardest person to understand is ourselves. It's like trying to read the label from inside the jar; we're just too close to get the full picture. This is where the power of perspective comes in—the ability to see ourselves through the eyes of others.

Reach out to your trusted friends and family and ask them a simple question:

"What do you think my superpower is?"

This isn't just about flattery or feel-good moments. It's a chance to uncover insights into your strengths and unique abilities that you might have overlooked or undervalued. The value of this exercise lies in its ability to reveal hidden facets of your character and capabilities. Often, others observe qualities in us that we take for granted or don't recognize as special. This feedback is like a mirror reflecting our best traits and skills, helping us understand our true potential and how we can leverage it.

Go ahead and have these conversations. You might be surprised to find that what others see as your superpower could be something you've never considered your strength. These insights can become a cornerstone in understanding how to present yourself to the world.

STEP 2: IDENTIFY THE SEVEN MAJOR HEADACHES YOU SOLVE

What pain points do you tackle? If you're scratching your head over this, simply use what I call the Seven Major

Headaches exercise. Think through the things that the people you serve lose sleep over. This doesn't have to be a perfectly worded list of things but rather general concepts you can pull from when needed.

In fact, I did this very exercise again when crafting the outline for this book. Thinking about the Seven Major Headaches of small-business owners, I came up with this rough outline:

1. Not sure what they really want their business to do for them.
2. Frustrated because they don't have a plan to get financially free.
3. Feel alone and don't know who they need on their team.
4. Don't know how to expand their network.
5. Don't know what to do with the money they've already earned.
6. Worry what would happen to their business if they get sick or pass away.
7. Wonder what habits and mindset they need to develop to make and keep millions.

This exercise will help you connect more deeply with the people you help and those who know the people you help.

STEP 3: DETERMINE THE COST OF NOT HIRING (OR KNOWING) YOU

While the first two steps might seem straightforward, this next one often goes overlooked: determine the cost of not hiring (or knowing) you. In other words, what does someone lose by not opting for your product or service? What do they miss out on by not being connected to you and your network?

Understanding the cost of not hiring you is a game-changer in many industries. A few straightforward examples: Without a health or wellness coach, individuals might continue detrimental habits, leading to increased medical costs and poorer quality of life. Imagine a wellness coach saying, "Without my guidance, you risk ongoing health challenges and higher future health-care costs."

A digital marketing expert might point out, "By neglecting your digital marketing, you're overlooking a massive audience, potentially costing you a substantial increase in customers."

An IT security consultant can make it clear: "Without expert security, your business is open to costly cyber threats."

Real estate agents can help potential homeowners avoid overpaying or missing critical property faults. They might say, "Navigating the property market alone can lead to overpaying or buying a problematic home. I will ensure you get the best deal."

Each of these examples highlights the significant impact of professional services and the potential risks and losses of going it alone. But let's take things a step further. Think about all the great people you have in your network. How many of them have you referred to others? How many times have you been asked, "Hey, I'm looking for a _____, do you know anyone?"

If you've ever moved to a new city or country where you don't know anyone, think about how many people you do *not* know—you're starting from scratch! Not only are you looking for a doctor, dentist, mechanic, plumber, or babysitter, you're not even sure who you could meet for lunch or where to go grocery shopping.

Many business owners feel the same way about their business network. They don't have an accountant, or someone to build their website, or a salesperson, or someone who understands social media. They aren't sure who to talk to about investing or legacy planning or real estate. This is exactly why so many of my clients over the years have come through word of mouth.

This will sound like a mouthful, but people trust the people their trusted people trust. This is the network you have access to that others don't. Make that list and you'll start to see just how valuable you and your network could be to others.

STEP 4: HELP OTHERS HELP YOU

Most business owners would gladly take a great referral, but the key to getting them is making it easy for others to refer you. Guide your promoters and give them the words to use when talking about you. Better yet, utilize a strategy to make this even easier.

I learned an example of this concept from a childhood favorite movie. In *Willy Wonka & the Chocolate Factory*, Willy Wonka, the eccentric owner of the chocolate factory, announces that he has hidden five golden tickets in random Wonka Bars. Anyone who finds one of these tickets gains entrance to the factory for a special tour and a chance to win a lifetime supply of chocolate. The golden ticket represents a rare and exciting opportunity for the characters in the story, particularly for Charlie, the impoverished protagonist, whose discovery of the final ticket changes his life forever.

That's exactly what we introduced in my company years ago, a "Golden Ticket" for our clients. This strategy completely changed the trajectory of my business.

The Golden Ticket Strategy

A strong network is like a garden—it requires consistent nurturing. When you introduce with intent, then every connection has a purpose. Knowing this, my team and I were brainstorming about how to get more referrals. Getting referrals is tough, especially in industries like mine, where privacy is king. We decided to give each client two "Golden Tickets" a year. Why just two tickets? Limiting the number heightened the value. Plus, it made our clients really think about who they'd like to share this privilege with.

These tickets offered something valuable for free, exclusively for the people our clients cared about most. Like attracts like. Our clients' networks were filled with similar-minded folks, potentially our ideal customers. By making these tickets scarce and exclusive, we created a buzz. Our clients felt special and were more inclined to share these tickets with their most valued contacts. They felt great talking about us because it elevated their relationships with the people they referred to us. It wasn't just any referral; it was a golden opportunity—both for us and for the receiver.

Get creative and think about how you can make it effortless for your clients to refer others. If you're short on ideas, try the Golden Ticket strategy with just a handful of your best customers. A referral isn't just a business transaction; it's an endorsement of trust. By making it a win-win, you not only grow your business but also deepen your relationship with existing clients.

STEP 5: CRAFT YOUR PERFECT PITCH

When it comes to crafting a pitch, there are tons of exercises and frameworks out there. I like to keep things simple because while I can craft a pitch, it often comes out differently in the context of a conversation. Don't feel pressured to get this down word for word. Think of it less as something you memorize and more something that you communicate.

I have several pitches because I worked in a few different sectors, but generally the goal in all my pitches is to address a problem, offer a plan, and promise a result.

For example, I start with the pain point of business owners being trapped in their business, offer the Freedom Plan, and promise the reward of more time, money, and a richer life. A few more examples from a few different industries (and one nonprofit):

- Most financial advisers struggle to sell life insurance. We remove the hassle of long paperwork, the awkwardness of asking health questions, and the delay in compensation.
- Many Ugandan children suffer from HIV, poverty, and don't get more than one meal a day. Our shelter provides healthy food, top-shelf medical care, and education so they can have the life they deserve.

- We help families struggling to navigate the process of Medicaid. Our firm helps you get qualified and protect at least half of what's yours.

All of these showcase a problem, plan, and result, but they can be a mouthful and sound a bit forced in real-life conversation. I've come a long way since practicing my introductions in the aisles of Kmart, and one of the most helpful things I learned was to keep it simple and memorable.

I simply tell people, "I help business owners make and keep more money." If you're an accountant, you could shift your introduction from "I'm an accountant" to "I help people fire their worst business partner: the IRS." See the difference?

This will take a bit of work, but if you go through the five steps I've given you, you'll gain a ton of clarity on what you bring to the table and how you can utilize more effective and powerful introductions.

THOU SHALT FOLLOW UP WITHIN FORTY-EIGHT HOURS

In the world of networking and building relationships, timing is everything. Following up within forty-eight hours after an introduction or meeting is a crucial step in cementing a new connection. It's the sweet spot where the interaction is still fresh in both parties' minds. Delaying follow-ups can lead to missed opportunities because the momentum from your initial meeting fades.

Remember, the fortune is in the follow-up. Every interaction you have is an opportunity to build a bridge or strengthen a bond. By ensuring that you reconnect within forty-eight hours, you're making a statement about your reliability and dedication. Following up is an integral part of that winning strategy, turning brief encounters into lasting connections. I always imagined bumping into the perfect client while browsing at Kmart. If I did, I had my next moves planned: get their contact info and continue following up! Invite them for coffee or a chat.

To sum up, mastering your introduction is about more than just stating your name and job title. It's about creating a connection, showing the value you bring, and painting a picture of what others miss out on without your service. Time to refine your introduction. It's a crucial step in making sure you're not just heard but remembered.

KEY TAKEAWAYS

- Your network needs to be a "net that works."
- Cast vision, remove friction, and build bridges.
- "In the business world, unfortunately, the rearview mirror is always clearer than the windshield."

- A single introduction can open doors that seemed locked forever.
- "Networking is more about farming than it is about hunting."
- The fortune is in the follow-up.

LET'S GO DEEPER

Go to liveliferichbook.com, download and print the guide, and start working through these exercises. Or simply grab a journal, jot down the date, and work through these questions.

- Ask your trusted friends and colleagues, "What is my superpower?"
- Identify the Seven Major Headaches your primary customer faces.
- Jot down the names of people you have referred others to in order to get a sense of the strength of your own network.
- Consider implementing the Golden Ticket strategy to have your best customers refer you to others. Can you see the benefits of doing this? Why or why not?
- Use the examples given as templates for you to craft a pitch around the plan, promise, and result you offer.

5

Make Money Your Best Employee

Years ago I was working with a business owner whose story was a real eye-opener. She poured her life savings into her business, which, after twelve years, was thriving and expanding nationwide. However, when she fell ill, the lack of a solid fallback plan hit hard. She never considered building an emergency fund for the business for a potential disability or critical illness. Suddenly, she found herself needing to pay someone else to fill her role, a role that no one could truly match in terms of passion and commitment.

Most business owners would love to be in the situation my client was in—until she got sick. She had her sales, marketing, financials, and operations down. She was meeting regularly with her accountants, advisers, and attorneys. But she neglected to think seriously about protection in the event of disability, and because most of her money was put right back into her business, she ended up in a very vulnerable situation.

At the end of this chapter there will be a link to a downloadable checklist called the Entrepreneur Assessment. This is a list of simple yes/no questions that I ask all of my clients to work through. I urge you to do the same before you go on to the next chapter. You've learned enough about the basics to answer these questions accurately and also see what you still need to work through. Remember, the end goal is to get you to a place of financial freedom through your business. Financial freedom is all about being prepared for the "no matter what." You don't have to wait until your business reaches a certain level to start planning for the potential of something happening to you.

Now, let's talk about the three buckets you need to fill in order to build toward financial freedom.

THE THREE-BUCKET STRATEGY FOR POSITIONING YOUR PROFITS

What do you do with the money your business is making? Is there a strategy in place so that you are setting aside your hard-earned profits? Many folks build a business in hopes of freedom but end up building a prison of their own making. While it may sound good to just reinvest all your profits back into the business, my advice is to position your profits.

To truly get financially free, you have to make your money work for you. Create three financial buckets for your business: short-term, intermediate, and legacy. This will help you make your money your best employee. Let's take a deeper look at each of them.

Short-Term Bucket
(taxable, for use over the next two years)

This bucket is for immediate or near-future needs. It's about having readily accessible funds for short-term goals, emergencies, or opportunities that may arise. This could include a cash emergency fund for your business to cover unexpected expenses or opportunities that require quick action.

Money in this bucket is accessible and flexible but is subject to current tax rates. Think of your regular business earnings, personal savings, or brokerage accounts. Here, you can quickly move money for immediate opportunities or needs, but you also need to keep an eye on the tax implications of your investments and earnings.

Intermediate Bucket
(tax deferred and won't touch for the next three to ten years)

This bucket focuses on mid-term goals and needs. It's about setting aside funds for objectives that are a few years away but not in the distant future.

This category includes investments like traditional IRAs or 401(k)s, where your contributions grow tax-free until you withdraw them, typically in retirement. This deferral allows your investments to compound over time without the drag of annual taxes, potentially leading to more substantial growth.

Marissa Nehlsen

3 Buckets to Position Your Profits Worksheet

Income - Expenses = Profit

Short-Term
Less Than 2 years

Quick Access
3-6 Month Expenses
Liquid & Safe

Short-Term Needs
(E.g., Cash Emergency, Vacation, Cash for Personal/Business)

_____ $_____
_____ $_____
_____ $_____
_____ $_____
_____ $_____
_____ $_____

Intermediate Term
2-10 years

Low Risk
Specific Amounts
Liquid & Safe

Intermediate Term
(E.g., Big Purchase, New Vehicle, College Fund, New Home)

_____ $_____
_____ $_____
_____ $_____
_____ $_____
_____ $_____
_____ $_____

Legacy
10+ years

Risk vs Reward
How Long Will It Last
How Much Will You Need

Legacy
(E.g., Taxable, Tax Deferred, Tax Exempt)

_____ $_____
_____ $_____
_____ $_____
_____ $_____
_____ $_____
_____ $_____

LIVE LIFE RICH www.marissanehlsen.com

Legacy Bucket
(tax exempt, won't touch for ten years and beyond)

The legacy bucket is about long-term planning and future goals. This category includes investments like Roth IRAs, where you contribute after-tax money, but your withdrawals, including the earnings, are tax-free under certain conditions.

By strategically placing your investments across these three buckets, you're preparing for various stages of your business's growth. This approach ensures that every dollar you earn, save, or invest works within the framework of your overall financial goals and tax strategy.

YOU NEED MORE THAN ONE RAINMAKER

The term *rainmaker* originated from Native American traditions, referring to individuals who possessed the ability to conjure rain during times of drought. In business, a rainmaker is someone who brings in money, much like bringing rain to dry land.

Chances are you have been your own rainmaker more times than not. The key is to make sure you're not the only rainmaker working to fill your three buckets. It's hard to just earn and grind your way to financial freedom. You need other sources that go beyond what only you can do.

There are three categories where you should invest your money:

- **First, invest in your own business:** This is where you pour your heart, soul, and resources, aiming to transform all your effort into profit. You'll want to create a team that frees you up to create additional income streams for the business (we'll cover this more in depth later) and eventually work yourself out of the business.
- **Second, invest in other businesses:** This refers to stocks, bonds, or other investments like partnerships. It's about spreading your wings and putting your money where it can grow, benefiting from dividends and capital gains.
- **Third, real estate:** No matter how you feel about it, real estate is a classic and powerful way to build wealth. Whether it's through rental properties or owning the building where your business operates, real estate can provide a steady stream of residual income. Investing in real estate isn't mandatory when it comes to financial freedom, but it's worth considering.

Note that many real estate owners are just one extended vacancy away from real trouble. One path forward is to primarily focus on funding your business and investments, then set aside a remaining percentage for real estate. Obviously that comes with risk, and one of the most common pitfalls has to do with running out of cash flow or not having enough cash on hand.

These strategies integrate with the three buckets we talked about earlier—short-term, intermediate, and legacy. It's a beautiful thing when you have both rain and the buckets to catch the downpour. Money set aside in these buckets serves as a reservoir for future investment and growth.

So how long will it really take to see a return? Let's look at the Rule of 72.

THE RULE OF 72

The Rule of 72 is a nifty little formula that helps you figure out how quickly your investments can double.

72 ÷ Rate of Return = Years to Double Investment

Let's say you have an investment or a savings account and you're curious about its growth potential. Simply divide the interest rate into 72, and voilà, you've got the number of years it will take for your money to double.

For instance, if you're earning a 10 percent return, divide that into 72, and you're looking at your money doubling every 7.2 years.

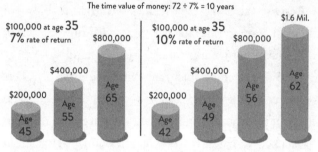

Using this rule, we can see how different rates of return impact the growth of an initial investment of $100,000:

$100,000 at age 35 with a 7 percent rate of return

- At age 45: The investment grows to $200,000.
- At age 55: The investment grows to $400,000.
- At age 65: The investment grows to $800,000.

$100,000 at age 35 with a 10 percent rate of return

- At age 42: The investment grows to $200,000.
- At age 49: The investment grows to $400,000.
- At age 56: The investment grows to $800,000.
- At age 62: The investment grows to $1.6 million.

This simple yet powerful rule underscores the importance of the rate of return on your investments. Now, let's talk about reality. If your savings account is growing at a snail's pace, say 2 percent, it's going to take a whopping thirty-six years for your money to double.

If you're fifty or sixty today, you probably won't want to wait thirty-six years to double your money. It's not enough to build substantial wealth, nor is it adequate for setting up the next generation for success.

You may be getting started on filling these buckets a little bit later in life, but if you're in a high-growth industry where you can make lots of money quickly, you might be able to gain financial ground by being more aggressive.

For example, I have several friends and colleagues who are in consulting and they aren't bound to any standards for what they can charge per project. Some are able to create multiple income streams around their intellectual property without putting more time into their work, say by publishing a book, white-labeling their curriculums to companies, or selling online courses. They typically don't have the large amounts of overhead that other small-business owners have to deal with because of rent, utilities, and employees at their brick-and-mortar locations.

They can make a lot of money and may continue to work long hours by choice and choose to invest their profits in the market rather than be bound to investing in and managing property, which may take up a lot of their time and brain power that could be better utilized in growing their consulting revenue streams.

Every situation is different, but what ties everything together regardless of the kind of business you run is that you need the three buckets and a plan to make it rain in order to fill them.

CAN'T I JUST SELL MY BUSINESS TO BE FINANCIALLY FREE?

Selling your business is a way to build wealth, but there are many factors you need to take into consideration. To start, most business owners don't think about assessing the true value of their business until they consider selling. Thinking about this value, known as *valuation*, when you're about to sell is way too late to do this. You need to think about valuation much, much earlier.

If things ever take a downturn, you want to make sure the value of your business doesn't plummet because of a hasty, distressed sale—often known as a *fire sale*. If you're unfamiliar with the term, it's when you're forced to sell something quickly, usually due to unexpected circumstances and often at a much lower value. In fire sales, buyers take advantage of your urgency, offering less than what your business or property is truly worth.

Having a thorough business valuation is not just about putting a price tag on your business; it's about understanding its true worth in various scenarios—be it a potential sale, an unforeseen IRS audit, or if one of your partners needs to exit the business. A valuation takes into account various factors, including underlying systems, processes, customer base, and market position. It gives you a clear picture of where a business stands and its potential worth to a prospective buyer. This valuation is essential when you need to execute a buy-sell agreement.

THE FIVE P'S: HOW TO EVALUATE NEW OPPORTUNITIES

For every new initiative I've taken, I always run through what I call the Five P's. This is a lens through which I view my ventures—a structured way of thinking and a framework to guide every decision. This is crucial because I've noticed that even the most talented entrepreneurs might excel in one or two areas but often miss out on others, including me.

As you look at your current business or any future ventures you might start, remember to view them through this lens:

- Purpose and Passion
- Plan
- People
- Processes
- Pricing for Profit

Let's touch on these quickly. They will overlap somewhat with what we've already covered in the book so far, but I'm categorizing them this way so you can quickly recall a framework to evaluate opportunities that come your way.

I want you to be equipped to see the entire picture rather than get blinded by shiny opportunities. If an opportunity passes these five filters, it might be worth considering. If not, it might be one you'll want to pass up.

Purpose and Passion

Why are you looking at this new business or venture? If you're in it just for the money, you might want to rethink things. Sure, making money is great, but do you have an understanding of this kind of business and a passion for it that will help you power through the hard times that inevitably come with any business or opportunity?

If it's something that is completely outside the realm of your current expertise or doesn't align with your vision for life, then your decision might be easier than you think. If you're a business consultant like several of my friends I mentioned earlier, buying a new chain of laundromats might be something you really need to think through. If you love to travel but these laundromats are all located in a city you'd never want to live in, let alone visit, rethink it. Remember, when the vision is clear, the decisions are easy.

I believe we all have a gift, something special we're good at. Find that thing, and use it to serve others in your unique way. Write it down, stick it on your bathroom mirror: "This is why I run my business. This is why I get up every day." When the going gets tough, this reminder is what will keep you pushing forward.

Plan

As the old saying goes, "If you fail to plan, then you plan to fail." Every truly successful business owner, entrepreneur, and investor understands the importance of a solid plan. Answer these basic but crucial questions:

- How will this business or venture make money?
- Who is the intended customer?
- What problem does it solve?
- What is its competitive advantage?
- How much can I expect to make, and how soon?
- Who will run it?
- What is my exit plan?

You need to have this nailed down before you even think about launching.

People

We covered a bit about your Freedom Team in an earlier chapter, but for this context you really need to be sure about the folks working on this business or opportunity. Do they have a proven track record? Are they finishers?

Do they keep promises? Will you simply be an investor, or will you work alongside others in a more hands-on role?

Many business owners are surprised at how much they need to grow as leaders of people rather than masters of their craft when it comes to growing a business. This really is where the rubber meets the road. You need to identify the roles that are crucial for your business growth and focus on attracting individuals who can fill these roles effectively.

Oftentimes, this means replacing you in a role that you may have taken on in order to get the business off the ground. This might mean looking beyond the allure of contractors and considering full-time, dedicated professionals who can invest their time and energy into your business.

This is where your business culture, vision, and values play an integral role. Top talents are often attracted to environments where they can grow, contribute meaningfully, and align with the business's vision. But attracting talent is just part of the equation. Retaining them is equally, if not more, critical. This is where you need to think about creating an engaging and supportive work environment.

Processes

Have you ever wondered what makes brands like McDonald's so successful worldwide? It's all about their processes. No matter where you go, whether it's a McDonald's in the heart of New York or halfway across the world in Tokyo, the experience and quality are pretty similar.

Good processes can really make your day-to-day operations smoother and are the playbook every team member follows. Who will ensure that everyone knows their role, reduces mistakes, and keeps things running without a hitch? Are the processes in this business scalable and transferable into new locations and markets? Does it have a plug-and-play capacity?

A few book recommendations for you that dive deeper into this particular topic: *The E-Myth Revisited*[9] and *The 4 Disciplines of Execution*.[10] They're fantastic for understanding how to create effective processes and set achievable goals in your business.

Pricing for Profit

Entrepreneur Jeff Bezos once said, "Your margin is my opportunity." Bezos implied that areas where existing businesses are making high profit margins are opportunities for new players to enter the market, potentially through acquisitions. You need to be clear on what these margins are when looking at starting or acquiring a new business or venture.

Profit margin is just one thing potential buyers look for when considering buying a business. If someone has reached a point where selling the business seems like the best option, then you should know what it is truly worth. Whether you decide to buy into a new venture or sell yours, each of these five P's should be taken into account.

KEY TAKEAWAYS

- Financial freedom is all about being prepared for the "no matter what."
- Build the three buckets for positioning your profits: short-term, intermediate, and legacy.
- You need more than one rainmaker.
- To calculate how quickly you can double your investments, use the Rule of 72: simply divide the interest rate into 72.
- Evaluate new opportunities through the lens of the Five P's: Purpose, Plan, People, Processes, and Profit.

LET'S GO DEEPER

Go to liveliferichbook.com to download the free workbook and take the Entrepreneur Assessment.

6

8 Streams of Income Every Entrepreneur Should Consider

Most of us are familiar with the online retail giant Amazon. Amazon started as an online bookstore and then grew into the "everything store" we all know today. But there's a part of their story that's super interesting and important to consider. It's about their cloud computing service, Amazon Web Services (AWS for short), and how it turned into an unexpected yet massive success.

As Amazon was expanding they needed a strong and flexible IT system to handle their growing online store. They built a system themselves and then had an aha moment: they realized that the technology they created wasn't just useful for them. Other companies were struggling with the same issues and could use a service like the one Amazon had just created.

In 2006, Amazon decided to offer their in-house AWS solution to other businesses. Now, AWS is a giant in the cloud computing world. It's a massive revenue stream for Amazon, sometimes making more money than their retail store.[11] What started as a side project to support their main business became a powerhouse on its own. Amazon's AWS adventure shows us that diversifying income streams can become an unexpected jackpot.

In the last chapter we talked about making money work for you and a framework of questions to consider *before* diving into new opportunities. In this chapter, we'll cover why you *should* consider opportunities that can add revenue streams. Here are a few reasons to consider new streams of income:

- **A Financial Safety Net:** Ever been caught off guard by life events? We all have. Having multiple income streams serves as a safety net under your financial high-wire act. One stream might falter but you won't hit the ground.
- **Accelerating Your Wealth Journey:** If wealth is a destination, relying on one income stream is like taking the scenic route: it's not the quickest way to get where you want to go. Diversifying your income can be like hopping on a financial expressway so you can reach your savings and investment goals way faster.

- **Harnessing Opportunities:** The world is like a treasure chest of opportunities, but you need to be ready to explore like Amazon did. With multiple income streams, you're not just stuck with one map; you've got several to choose from.

Creating multiple income streams isn't just for the wealthy. It's how many people became wealthy to begin with. Let's start with breaking down income streams into two big categories: active and passive income.

ACTIVE AND PASSIVE INCOME

Understanding the distinction between active and passive income is crucial for building a robust financial strategy. This graphic highlights the differences and considerations for both types of income, helping you identify and optimize your income sources effectively.

Income Producing Activities

Active vs. Passive Income

Active Income	Passive Income
• Requires You • Your Business • Product, Hybrid, Service	Consider the Three R's • What is **Required**? • Where is my greatest **Reward**? • What is my **Return**? **Examples:** • Stock Market • Real Estate

Active Income

Active income is the money you earn by actively participating in your business or job. This type of income requires your direct involvement and effort. Examples include:

- **Your Business:** If you own a business, the profits you earn from its operations.
- **Products, Services, and Hybrid Models:** Selling products, offering services, or a combination of both.

Active income is essential, but it often requires ongoing effort and time commitment.

Passive Income

Passive income, on the other hand, is earned with minimal effort. Once the initial setup is complete, it requires little to no daily involvement. Examples of passive income include the stock market, real estate, and royalties. We'll dig into this further later in this chapter.

THE THREE R'S OF INCOME

As you venture into the world of diversifying income streams, there are three pivotal questions to guide your journey that I call the Three R's: *required*, *return*, and *reward*.

- **What is required of me?** This is about understanding the investment of time, energy, and money needed for each income stream. It's crucial to evaluate what you're willing to commit to get each income source up and running and keep it profitable. Is it something that requires constant attention, or can it grow with minimal oversight?
- **Where is my greatest return?** While some avenues might offer higher returns, it's wise to spread your investments across different areas. I often think back to lessons from working on the farm with my grandparents: never put all your eggs in one basket. Diverse income sources mean you're not left vulnerable if one area faces a downturn. Think about various scenarios: What if rental properties face unexpected vacancies or stock market fluctuations affect your investments? Spreading your resources across the eight income streams outlined later in this chapter can create a more stable financial foundation.
- **Where do I get my greatest reward?** This is about what brings you joy and satisfaction. Which income streams align with your passions and interests? What excites you about the process, not just the profit? This is about finding fulfillment in your financial endeavors, not just accumulating wealth.

Take a moment to reflect on these questions. Assess where you currently stand and how you can evolve toward a more diversified, fulfilling, and profitable financial future. Remember, it's not just about the destination; it's also about enjoying the journey and finding purpose in your financial growth.

To further help you identify and optimize your income sources, download the Sources for Cash Flow Worksheet at liveliferichbook.com. This worksheet will guide you through the process of categorizing your income sources and evaluating them based on the Three R's, enabling you to create a balanced and sustainable financial strategy.

8 TYPES OF INCOME STREAMS

Now let's explore the different types of income streams and how to strategically integrate them into your Freedom Plan.

1. Earned Income

Earned income is the paycheck from your day job. It's what most of us are familiar with, where someone else determines our pay and hours. Most people rely on earned income. You work, get paid, and save a little for yourself.

2. Profit Income

Profit income essentially comes from buying and selling. Think about the process of fixing and flipping a house. You buy it, spruce up the property, then sell it for more money. It's a straightforward formula: income minus expenses equals profit. This is a great way to create cash flow but requires a keen eye for opportunities and smart investment choices.

3. Interest Income

This is what you earn from lending money. Traditionally, people think of this as a savings or money market account. While these are common ways to earn interest, it's crucial to weigh them against current economic factors, like inflation and changing interest rates.

Recently, we've seen a significant shift in both interest rates and inflation. When prime rates jump they can present a challenge for new entrepreneurs or young families just starting out. When you're dealing with interest income, always consider whether your returns are genuinely increasing your wealth or merely keeping pace with inflation.

Remember, two things can significantly impact your profits: taxes and inflation. *Inflation* refers to the rising cost of goods and services over time and it can silently erode your savings. When exploring interest-income opportunities, always consider the broader economic landscape and how it affects your real earning potential.

4. Residual Income

This is where you continue to get paid even after the work is done. Imagine having a business or investment that keeps generating income, even when you're not actively involved in the day-to-day operations. That's residual income.

Let me give you an example. I have a business-savvy friend who specializes in 1031 real estate exchanges. Instead of charging an hourly or fixed rate for his services, he negotiates a percentage of the long-term profits of the real estate deals he orchestrates. He brings together all necessary parties: accountants, attorneys, and the capital needed to close deals. Once the deal is done he stays on as a silent partner, continuing to earn a percentage of the real estate's ongoing income. This is residual income in action: do the work once, set up the deal, and continue to earn from it over time.

Now, let's talk about my personal experience with residual income. I own several businesses, and in most of them, my involvement is now minimal. In one of these businesses, I don't draw a regular salary or hourly pay. Instead, I receive what's known as a K-1 distribution: a share of the profits. After subtracting all the business expenses, including employee salaries and overhead costs, the net profit is divided among the owners. So if a business makes $300,000 in net income and there are two partners with a fifty-fifty split, each partner gets a check for $150,000. That's their share of the profit, a classic example of residual income.

Residual income allows you to step back and still reap the benefits of your initial hard work and investment. This situation is my hope for nearly all of my small-business clients and friends: that their team, systems, and business would be set up enough to run without them while they collect residual income.

5. Dividend Income

Dividends are your earnings from owning stocks. When a stock in your portfolio performs well, it can pay dividends. This is essentially a portion of the company's profits distributed to shareholders. Remember, with dividends, there's a tax aspect you need to be aware of. Unless your investments are in a tax-sheltered account, you're likely to pay taxes even if you reinvest them or don't withdraw them.

Dividend income is essentially a reward for your investment savvy. It's a way for the stock market to thank you for investing in a company. Keep in mind, dividend income is not just about enjoying those quarterly or annual payouts; it's also about understanding and managing their impact on your overall financial portfolio.

6. Rental Income

This is money earned from renting out property, commercial or residential. I'm currently juggling a mix of these, including Airbnb properties. Rental income is a fantastic source of cash flow. However, you must consider the logistics of managing these properties. Who will handle maintenance? Who's overseeing the day-to-day operations? In my case, I've set things up to be fairly passive. It doesn't eat into my daily schedule, but it still needs occasional oversight, and, of course, I must take my expenses into account.

7. Capital Gains

This is profit from selling an asset that has increased in value. Here's a straightforward example: Imagine you bought a property for $150,000, and now it's worth $250,000. If you decide to sell, you have capital gains: the $100,000 profit you've made on that investment.

Typically, you're liable for capital gains tax on such transactions. This is where having a good accountant becomes crucial—they'll help you navigate the tax implications based on your specific situation. Capital gains are a way to build wealth over time, but (you guessed it) it's important to be aware of the tax responsibilities that come with these gains.

8. Royalty Income

Royalty income refers to the money earned from the use of one's intellectual property or other assets. It's commonly associated with payments made for the use of copyrighted material, such as books, music, and patents. Royalties are often paid to creators of intellectual property, like authors, musicians, inventors, and software developers. Payments are usually made based on the usage of the property. For example, a musician might receive a fee each time their song is played on the radio or a writer might earn a percentage of each book sold.

There are various types of royalties, such as mechanical royalties (from the reproduction of copyrighted musical compositions), performance royalties (from the public performance of copyrighted works), and patent royalties (from the use of a patented invention). Royalties are often paid for the duration of the copyright or patent, which can be many years. Because of this, royalty income is considered a form of passive income, as it can continue to generate earnings long after the initial creation of the work.

Overall, royalty income provides a way for creators and inventors to earn money from their creations over time, rewarding them for their original work.

The good news is that if you start and run a business, you can generate enough money and means to build all of these income streams much faster than someone who has only earned income.

KEY TAKEAWAYS

- Understand the distinction between active and passive income.
- Think about the Three R's: required, return, and reward.
- Consider the eight streams of income:
    1. Earned income: income from a job
    2. Profit income: income from buying and selling things
    3. Interest income: income from lending money
    4. Residual income: getting paid after the work is done
    5. Dividend income: income from owning stocks
    6. Rental income: income from renting out property

7. Capital gains: making money when selling an appreciated asset
8. Royalty income: getting paid when others use or purchase your intellectual property

LET'S GO DEEPER

To further help you identify and optimize your income sources, download the Sources for Cash Flow Worksheet at liveliferichbook.com. This worksheet will guide you through the process of categorizing your income sources and evaluating them based on the Three R's, enabling you to create a balanced and sustainable financial strategy.

Fire Your Worst Business Partner: The Tax Collector

There are two tax codes: one for those who are informed and the other for the uninformed. Both are legal.

We've all heard the saying that it's not about how much money you make; it's how much you keep. Let's take this a step further: every dollar paid in taxes is a dollar less for your long-term plans and dreams. For small-business owners, every penny counts. You've likely experienced sleepless nights, financial uncertainties, and the stress of balancing growing bills with limited resources. Cutting down on unnecessary tax expenditures isn't just about saving money; it's about smart financial planning and ensuring that the fruits of your hard work and sacrifice are maximized for you. In other words, you need to learn how to fire the worst business partner you'll ever have: the tax collector.

Every country in the world requires some form of taxes to be paid. Knowing your options on deductions, credits, and so forth is key to taking control of your financial future. This is going to be a meaty chapter and it's one you should come back to time and again. Learning about taxes isn't always fun, but it's lucrative. Remember, no one is going to care as much about your money or business as you.

Let's start with an example on how having the right tax strategy can yield a completely different outcome. While this is based on a situation in the United States, there are lessons that can be gleaned from this. Years ago I had two clients who were brothers and business partners. These brothers had worked hard to accumulate $3 million in equipment in their business. When it came time to sell their business, they were faced with a staggering 40 percent tax on the recaptured depreciation. This meant a potential tax bill of $1.2 million out of their $3 million, a significant chunk of their hard-earned profits.

They were understandably shocked.

Their $3 million in assets would suddenly be reduced to $1.8 million after taxes. Splitting it in half left each brother with only $900,000 after all the hard work they had done. Living off the interest of this amount, roughly $45,000 a year, was not feasible for them. They needed a plan, fast.

We decided on a plan to sell their business through a trust. This allowed them to avoid the $1.2 million tax hit and maintain the full $3 million. By keeping their funds in the trust, each brother could draw an annual income of $75,000 while paying income tax only on the money they withdrew each year. This is a powerful example of how strategic planning can dramatically alter the financial outcome of selling a business, turning a potentially devastating tax burden into a sustainable, long-term income stream.

Keep this story in mind as I'll explain this strategy at the end of this chapter.

WORKING FOR YOURSELF?

Another example from the United States: if you plan to work for yourself (freelancers, speakers, coaches, and consultants), then don't forget the self-employment tax. In 2024, this tax added another 15.3 percent on top of your regular tax rate. If you're sitting at a 22 percent tax bracket, add 15.3 percent, and you're giving away 37 percent of every dollar you earn to taxes—all before other taxes and expenses.

Navigating tax structures can be a significant challenge for self-employed individuals. This graphic illustrates the impact of different business structures on your tax liabilities, specifically focusing on the benefits of structuring your business as an LLC (limited liability company) taxed as an S corporation, compared to operating as a sole proprietor.

No matter where you are operating out of, this is why you need to meet with your attorney and tax adviser and ask if you are properly structured for the value of your business and whether the structure you're in is optimized so you can keep more of what you make. They should be able to run scenarios for you to see how the numbers slide and change depending on your situation. Take a look at this graphic, and I'll explain further.

Tax Structure for Self-Employed

Challenge: Sole Proprietor Schedule C or F	Solution: Structure Business to LLC (1120s)
Example: $100,000 Net Income -Self Employment Tax 15.3%	$50K - 15.3% Limited Liability Company (S Corp)
Social Security & Medicare Tax **$15,300**	**Social Security & Medicare Tax** **$7,650**

This is a hypothetical example and is not intended to predict or anticipate the actual result of any tax strategy.

As a sole proprietor, your business income is subject to self-employment tax, which includes Social Security and Medicare taxes.

For example, with a net income of $100,000, you would pay a self-employment tax rate of 15.3 percent, resulting in a tax liability of $15,300 solely for Social Security and Medicare.

However, by structuring your business as an LLC taxed as an S Corporation, you can reduce your self-employment tax liability. In this structure, you can take a portion of your income as salary (subject to self-employment tax) and the remainder as a distribution (not subject to self-employment tax).

For instance, if you take $50,000 as salary, you would pay the 15.3 percent self-employment tax on this amount, resulting in a tax liability of $7,650 for Social Security and Medicare. This effectively reduces your self-employment tax by half compared to the sole proprietor structure.

This isn't legal advice, so it's important to consult with your attorney and a tax professional to understand the best structure for your specific situation and to ensure compliance with all tax regulations. But this strategy is an example of one way that's available to optimize your tax situation and enhance your overall financial health.

THE FOUR BASIC RULES OF ALL EXPENSES

Understanding the basic rules of expenses is essential for navigating the complex world of taxes as a business owner. These rules serve as guidelines to ensure that your expenses are legitimate deductions that can help lower your taxable income.

1. The expenses must be incurred in connection with your trade, business, or profession.
2. The expenses must be "ordinary."
3. The expenses must be "necessary."

4. The expenses must "not be lavish" or "extravagant" under the circumstances.

Here's how they break down:

- **In connection with your trade, business, or profession:** This rule stipulates that expenses must be directly related to your business activities. Whether it's purchasing inventory, marketing your products or services, or renting office space, the expenses must have a clear connection to your trade, business, or profession.
- **"Ordinary" expenses:** An ordinary expense is one that is common and accepted in your industry or field of business. These are the expenses that other businesses similar to yours would typically incur. For example, office supplies, utilities, and wages for employees are considered ordinary expenses for many businesses.
- **"Necessary" expenses:** Necessary expenses are those that are helpful and appropriate for your business operations. They are expenses that are essential for the day-to-day functioning of your business and for generating income. This can include things like rent, utilities, equipment purchases, and professional services.
- **"Not lavish" or "extravagant":** This rule prevents you from deducting expenses that are considered extravagant or unnecessary. While it's

subjective, the IRS generally looks at whether the expense is reasonable and customary given the circumstances of your business. For example, a lavish business dinner at a high-end restaurant may not be fully deductible if it exceeds what is considered reasonable for a business meal.

By adhering to these basic rules, you can ensure that your business expenses are legitimate deductions that will withstand scrutiny from the IRS. This can help you maximize your tax savings while staying compliant with tax laws.

KEY COMPONENTS OF TAX PLANNING

Let's get a general overview of the key components of strategic tax planning. Strategic tax planning is an integral part of maintaining and growing your wealth. By focusing on these key areas, you can develop a comprehensive approach to managing your taxes effectively.

- **Qualified Retirement Plans:** Contributing to retirement plans like 401(k)s, IRAs, and other qualified plans can provide significant tax advantages. These plans often offer tax-deferred growth, allowing your investments to compound over time without the drag of annual taxes.
- **Charitable Giving:** Donations to charitable organizations can reduce your taxable income.

Strategic charitable giving not only supports causes you care about but also offers potential tax benefits.
- **Active vs. Passive Income:** Understanding the differences between active and passive income can help you optimize your tax strategy. Passive income sources often receive more favorable tax treatment, making them an essential part of a tax-efficient financial plan.
- **Income Tax Analysis:** Regularly reviewing your income tax situation can help you identify opportunities for tax savings. This includes analyzing your current tax bracket, deductions, credits, and other tax-saving strategies.
- **Succession/Transition Analysis:** Planning for the future of your business or estate involves considering the tax implications of succession and transitions. This ensures a smooth transfer of ownership or assets while minimizing tax burdens.
- **Estate-Tax Planning:** This involves preparing for the transfer of your wealth and assets to heirs or beneficiaries. Proper estate planning can minimize estate taxes, ensuring that more of your wealth is preserved for future generations.

We've been talking a lot about buckets and I want to show you one more set of buckets, this time to help you understand where the above components fit.

FIRE YOUR WORST BUSINESS PARTNER: THE TAX COLLECTOR

Strategic Tax Planning

Use this strategy to fire your worst business partner (The Tax Collector) and use your retirement plan to do it!

TAXABLE	TAX DEFERRED	TAX EXEMPT
For Example	For Example	For Example
• Rental Income • Social Security	• Simple IRA • Pension • IRA	• Roth • Roth IRA • Life Insurance

This is a hypothetical example and is not intended to predict or anticipate the actual result of any tax strategy.

Taxable Bucket

- Sources: rental income, Social Security
- Income in this bucket is subject to taxes in the year it is earned. This means any rental income or Social Security benefits you receive will be taxed according to your income bracket.
- Strategy: Manage the timing and amount of taxable income to optimize your overall tax liability each year.

Tax-Deferred Bucket

- Sources: simple IRA, pension, IRA
- Income in this bucket is not taxed when earned but is taxed when withdrawn, typically during

retirement. This allows the investments to grow tax-deferred.
- Strategy: Contribute to these accounts to reduce your current taxable income and take advantage of tax-deferred growth, potentially paying taxes at a lower rate upon withdrawal.

Tax-Exempt Bucket

- Sources: Roth IRA, life insurance
- Income in this bucket is not taxed at all, either when earned or withdrawn, as long as certain conditions are met. Contributions are made with after-tax dollars, but the growth and withdrawals are tax-free.
- Strategy: Invest in tax-exempt accounts to benefit from tax-free growth and withdrawals, providing a significant tax advantage in the long term.

THE MAGIC LINE ON YOUR TAX RETURN

There is a critical tax line on your 1040 form, specifically on schedule 1, part 2, line 16. Mastering this line can help you keep more of what you earn by maximizing your tax deductions and contributions to retirement plans.

The Exact Tax Lines

Secrets to Your "1040" - So you can keep more of what you make!

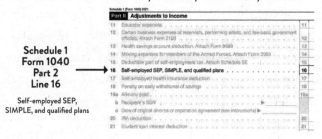

This line is where you report contributions to retirement plans such as SEP IRAs, SIMPLE IRAs, and other qualified plans. These contributions are crucial because they directly reduce your taxable income, lowering your overall tax liability. Here's why this matters:

- **Tax Savings:** Contributions to these retirement plans are tax-deductible, meaning they can significantly reduce your taxable income.
- **Retirement Security:** Investing in these plans ensures you are saving for retirement, providing financial security for the future.
- **Maximize Deductions:** Understanding and utilizing these exact tax lines can help you take full advantage of available deductions, ultimately keeping more of your hard-earned money.

By mastering the details of your 1040 form and focusing on key lines like line 16, you can ensure you are making the most of available tax deductions. This strategic approach not only saves you money in the short term but also sets you up for long-term financial stability. For small-business owners and self-employed individuals, leveraging these deductions is a powerful tool in your overall financial strategy.

UNDERSTANDING RETIREMENT PLAN OPTIONS

Navigating the world of retirement plans can be daunting, especially with so many options and regulations to consider. This section will provide a comprehensive overview of various retirement plan options to help you make informed decisions and maximize your financial future. There are two broad categories: (1) defined benefit plans (often known as pension plans) and (2) defined contribution plans (which include things like IRAs, SEPs, and more).

These will have different applications based on where you are in your journey. For example, if you still have a day job, your employer may already be funding your pension. If you are a business owner with employees, you may have set this up for your employees. Whatever the case, it's important to understand the broad overview of how all this works, so let's look at each and then take a deeper dive into the details.

DEFINED BENEFIT PLANS

Defined benefit plans, often referred to as pension plans, guarantee a specific retirement income amount to employees, providing a sense of security and stability. These plans are typically funded by employers who take on the investment risk instead of the employees, ensuring a fixed payout regardless of market performance. Employers make contributions to a fund, which is then used to pay out a predetermined amount to retirees based on factors such as salary history and length of employment.

- **Example:** A traditional pension plan where an employee receives a fixed monthly benefit upon retirement.
- **Key Benefit:** Provides a predictable income stream in retirement, ensuring financial security for employees.
- **Consideration for Employers:** Employers need to ensure adequate funding and management of the plan to meet future obligations.

DEFINED CONTRIBUTION PLANS

There are a number of defined contribution plans, some of which you've likely heard of. They include:

- Solo 401(k)
- Simplified employee pension (SEP)

- Traditional IRA
- Roth IRA
- Simple IRA
- 403(b) plans (for those working at nonprofit organizations)
- 457 plan (for those working at government agencies)

Defined contribution plans, with the most common example being a 401(k) plan, are retirement savings plans where employees and sometimes employers contribute to individual accounts for each participant. Employees are responsible for the amounts that are contributed. In these plans, employees design their own portfolio and manage their own investment risk, giving them more control over their retirement savings. Unlike defined benefit plans, the retirement income from defined contribution plans depends on the contributions made and the investment performance of those contributions.

For our purposes here, we'll bypass the plans for those working at nonprofit and government agencies. For the other plans, we'll cover some numbers that are current at the time of this writing, but I strongly encourage you to talk to your attorney and tax professional to look at the numbers for the year you're reading this and strategize to create the best approach for your situation.

- **Example:** 401(k) plans, where employees contribute a portion of their salary, often with matching contributions from their employer
- **Key Benefit:** Employees have control over their investment choices and contributions, offering flexibility and potential for growth.
- **Consideration for Employers:** Employers can offer matching contributions to incentivize employee savings and retention.

Solo 401(k) Plans

Designed for self-employed individuals with no employees, solo 401(k) plans allow for both employee and employer contributions, providing a powerful way to boost retirement savings.

- **Maximum Contribution:** Up to $70,000 per year, combining employee and employer contributions
- **Key Benefit:** High contribution limits and flexibility in contributions make it an excellent choice for maximizing retirement savings.
- **Ideal For:** Self-employed individuals and small-business owners who want to save aggressively for retirement

Simplified Employee Pension (SEP) Plans

SEP plans offer a simple and flexible way for small-business owners to contribute to their employees' retirement savings. Contributions are made directly to individual retirement accounts (IRAs) set up for each employee.

- **Contribution Rate:** Up to 25 percent of net income or a total contribution limit of $75,000, whichever is less.
- **Key Benefit:** Simplicity and flexibility make SEPs an attractive option for small-business owners who want to offer retirement benefits without complex administration.
- **Ideal For:** Self-employed individuals and small businesses looking for an easy-to-manage retirement plan

Individual Retirement Accounts (IRAs)

IRAs are personal savings plans that offer tax advantages for retirement savings. There are two main types of IRAs: Traditional IRAs and Roth IRAs.

Traditional IRA

- **Tax Treatment:** Contributions are tax-deductible, and earnings grow tax-deferred until withdrawn.

- **Withdrawal Rules:** Upon withdrawal in retirement, taxes are paid, typically at a lower rate than during working years, with withdrawals prior to age 59 1/2 incurring a 10 percent penalty.
- **Key Benefit:** Immediate tax deduction on contributions can lower your taxable income today.

Roth IRA

- **Tax Treatment:** Contributions are made with after-tax dollars, but earnings and withdrawals are tax-free in retirement.
- **Withdrawal Rules:** Contributions can be withdrawn at any time without penalty, and earnings can be withdrawn tax-free after age fifty-nine and a half.
- **Key Benefit:** Provides tax-free income in retirement, which can be especially beneficial if you expect to be in a higher tax bracket.

EMPLOYER-SPONSORED PLANS

Finally, let's cover the classic 401(k), which is "employee-sponsored." This means the 401(k) retirement savings plan is set up and offered by an employer to its employees as a benefit. Here are some key points to understand what this entails:

1. Employer Initiation and Administration

- **Setup:** The employer establishes the 401(k) plan and selects the financial institution or service provider to administer it. This includes setting up the plan structure, choosing the investment options available to employees, and ensuring the plan complies with regulatory requirements.
- **Administration:** The employer handles the administrative tasks associated with the plan, such as enrolling employees, managing contributions, and ensuring compliance with legal and tax regulations.

2. Employee Contributions

- **Payroll Deductions:** Employees can contribute a portion of their pre-tax—or after-tax, in the case of a Roth 401(k)—salary to their 401(k) account. These contributions are typically made through automatic payroll deductions.
- **Control over Contributions:** Employees decide how much they want to contribute to their 401(k), up to the annual contribution limit set by the IRS.

3. Employer Contributions

- **Matching Contributions:** Many employers choose to match a portion of the employee's contributions,

which is an additional benefit. For example, an employer might match 50 percent of employee contributions up to 6 percent of their salary.
- **Discretionary Contributions:** Some employers may also make discretionary contributions to the plan, providing additional funding to employees' retirement savings.

4. Investment Options

- **Selection:** The employer selects a range of investment options for the plan, such as mutual funds, stocks, bonds, and other financial instruments.
- **Employee Choice:** Employees can choose how to allocate their contributions among these investment options based on their individual retirement goals and risk tolerance.

5. Vesting

- **Employee Contributions:** Employee contributions to their 401(k) are always 100 percent vested, meaning the employee owns these funds outright.
- **Employer Contributions:** Employer contributions may be subject to a vesting schedule, which means the employee gains ownership of the employer's contributions over a period of time.

6. Benefits and Flexibility

- **Tax Advantages:** Contributions to a traditional 401(k) are made with pre-tax dollars, reducing the employee's taxable income. Roth 401(k) contributions are made with after-tax dollars, but qualified withdrawals in retirement are tax-free.
- **Retirement Savings:** The plan encourages employees to save for retirement by providing a convenient, tax-advantaged way to accumulate funds over time.
- **Portability:** Employees can take their vested 401(k) balance with them when they change jobs, either by leaving it in the old employer's plan, rolling it over to a new employer's plan, or transferring it to an individual retirement account (IRA).

In summary, an employee-sponsored 401(k) plan is a retirement savings program set up and managed by an employer, allowing employees to contribute a portion of their salary to individual retirement accounts. Employers often match contributions and provide a selection of investment options, giving employees a valuable tool for saving for retirement.

Here Is How It Works

Defined Benefit - Pension
Annual contribution amounts are based off a plan funding formula, earnings, and your age.

Maximum Benefit: $280,000

Details:
- 3-5 Year Funding Required
- Withdraw After Age 59 1/2
- Multiple Investment Options
- Much Larger Contributions

Solo 401(k) - Defined Contribution
Based on a $100,000 salary

Employee Contribution:	$23,500
Employee Catch-Up (Age 50+)	$7,500
Employer Contribution:	$18,587*
	$49,587yr
Maximum Contribution	$77,500yr

Details:
- Very Flexible Contributions
- Withdraw After Age 59 1/2
- Multiple Investment Options

*This number will vary depending on the year and your situation. Use your advisors to determine the correct strategy. This is a hypothetical example and is not intended to predict or anticipate the actual result of any tax strategy.

You may feel a bit lost right now, and that's all right. This portion of the chapter is meant to be used as a reference point so that you can have an overview of the options and be prepared to work with your team in order to strategize the best options for you. Let's take a more detailed look at the numbers, as of 2025.

DEFINED BENEFIT—PENSION:

- **Maximum Benefit:** $280,000
- **Contribution Formula:** Annual contribution amounts are based on a plan funding formula, earnings, and your age.
- **Details:**
  - **Funding Requirement:** Typically requires a funding period of three to five years.
  - **Withdrawal Age:** You can start withdrawing after age fifty-nine and a half.

- **Investment Options:** Offers multiple investment options.
- **Contribution Limits:** Allows for much larger contributions compared to other plans.

DEFINED CONTRIBUTION—SOLO 401(K):

- **Maximum Contribution:** $77,500 per year
  - **Employee Contribution:** $23,000
  - **Employee Catch-Up (Age 50+):** $7,500
  - **Employer Contribution:** $46,500*
- **Details:**
  - **Flexible Contributions:** Very flexible contribution options.
  - **Withdrawal Age:** You can start withdrawing after age fifty-nine and a half.
  - **Investment Options:** Provides multiple investment options.

Both types of plans offer unique benefits and cater to different retirement needs. Understanding these options will help you make better decisions for your financial future.

---

*This number will vary depending on the year and your situation. Use your advisors to determine the correct strategy.

Now, let's look at the two types of defined contribution plans: SEP and Solo 401(k), or what we often refer to as Solo K for short.

The Two Types of Defined Contribution Plans: SEP and Solo K

Both SEP and Solo 401(k) plans offer powerful ways to boost retirement savings, each with unique benefits.

Solo 401(k) plans are designed for self-employed individuals with no employees (other than a spouse). They offer high contribution limits, combining both employee and employer contributions, and an additional catch-up contribution for those aged fifty and older.

SEPs provide simplicity and flexibility, especially for small-business owners. Solo 401(k) plans, on the other hand, allow for higher contribution limits, making them an excellent choice for maximizing retirement savings.

Defined Contribution Plans

*This number will vary depending on the year and your situation. Use your advisors to determine the correct strategy.
This is a hypothetical example and is not intended to predict or anticipate the actual result of any tax strategy.

Understanding these limits can help you maximize your retirement savings and take full advantage of tax benefits.

SEP (Simplified Employee Pension):

1. **Net Schedule F Income:** $100,000
2. **Contribution Rate:** 25 percent[*]
3. **Total Contribution:** $25,000

SEPs are ideal for self-employed individuals and small-business owners. They allow for significant contributions based on a percentage of net income, providing flexibility and potential tax advantages.

Solo 401(k):

- **Employee Contribution:** $23,500
- **Catch-Up Contribution (Age 50+):** $7,500
- **Employer Contribution:** $18,587[†]
- **Total Contribution:** $49,587[†]

Understanding these plans can help you choose the best option for your financial future, ensuring you make the most of your retirement contributions.

---

[*] If you're self-employed, your contributions are generally limited to 20 percent of your net income.

[†] This number will vary depending on the year and your situation. Use your advisors to determine the correct strategy.

TAX STRATEGIST VS. TAX PREPARER: A WORLD OF DIFFERENCE

Many folks end up paying more taxes than necessary simply because they're not informed or don't have the right tax professional on their team. This is where the distinction between a tax preparer and a tax strategist becomes crucial.

I may ruffle some feathers here but I'm willing to do so because my responsibility is to you and not to your accountant. When it comes to taxes, you need to figure out whether you are working with a tax preparer or a tax strategist. The difference: a tax preparer is the one you dump all your receipts and records on and they come back with a figure you owe. There's no real advice or strategy, just a straightforward calculation.

On the other hand, a tax strategist is like a detective diving into the nuances of your business. They can talk to you about retirement plans, growth strategies, and long-term shelters for your earnings. They will provide a strategy to reduce your annual tax burden. They'll brainstorm with you on how best to structure your income, whether it's taking a portion as a K-1 distribution versus a wage and how that plays into your tax scenario.

Don't settle for an accountant who just tells you what you owe. As an entrepreneur, you need someone who understands how to maximize your advantages when it comes to the tax code. As your business grows, taxes will continually eat away at what you take home unless you get proactive about your deductions. How can your second home, plane tickets, or business meetings in LA, New York, or Florida become deductible? These are the golden nuggets a tax strategist will help you unearth.

While we touched on having a capable tax professional on your Freedom Team in an earlier chapter, let me take you a bit deeper on the questions to ask when looking for one.

A few questions to consider asking:

- Do you act as my tax strategist, looking for savings opportunities, or just prepare the numbers based on my provided documentation?
- What are the top ten tax tips I should be aware of for my situation this year? Can you provide me with a list to review?
- Am I taking advantage of all legal deductions, write-offs, and tax sheltering vehicles available?
- How can my business structure, retirement planning, and investments be optimized to minimize taxes?
- What proactive steps do you advise to reduce what I owe?

If you're sitting there with just a tax preparer, then it's time to reconsider. Even if they're cheaper, they could end up costing you way more in the long run. Find someone aggressive who will defend your deductions and guide you through savvy strategies.

It's crucial to get taxes right from the start because messing up taxes, especially if you have employees, is a serious issue. What kinds of taxes should you be aware of? Income tax, state tax, sales tax, those pesky 941 payroll taxes. You don't want to land in hot water over something like payroll taxes. These are things you might end up discussing in a not-so-fun meeting with your accountant.

ARE YOU PAYING YOUR ADVISER TOO MUCH?

It's important to evaluate the costs associated with financial services and ensure you're getting the best value for your money. I encourage you to understand the fees you're paying for various financial services and to determine whether you might be overpaying.

Are You Paying Too Much? When to Ask

Understanding what your options and choices can be!
How do your investments fit into the big picture? Are they coordinated?

Here's a breakdown of the services above:

- **Investment Advisory Services:** These services provide personalized advice and recommendations for your investment portfolio. It's crucial to understand the fee structure and whether you are paying commission sales charges or a flat management fee.
- **Retirement Planning:** Planning for retirement often involves various fees and charges. Ensure you know what you are paying for retirement planning services and if those fees are in line with industry standards.
- **Asset Management:** Managing your assets involves operational expenses. Compare the fees for retail services (commission-based) versus institutional services (flat fee) to determine if you're overpaying. Retail often includes commission-sales charges, fees, and operating expenses. These costs can add up and might not always be transparent. Institutional services typically offer a flat management fee, which can be more straightforward and potentially more cost-effective.
- **Portfolio Review:** Regular reviews of your investment portfolio are necessary to ensure alignment with your financial goals. Understanding the costs involved in these reviews can help you decide if they are worth the service provided.
- **Impacts of Taxes & Inflation:** Taxes and inflation can significantly affect your investment returns. Assessing the advisory fees in light of

these impacts can give you a clearer picture of the net value of the services you are receiving.

USING A CHARITABLE TRUST

At the start of this chapter I shared the story of the two brothers who were looking to sell their business but were worried about taxes. Many of my clients run into this situation, especially because they're in farming and ranching where even selling equipment can result in significant tax liabilities.

Here's a quick graphic on how we use a charitable trust to ensure the money stays in the family.

Tax Considerations: Equipment Auctions

I am considering an equipment auction, but I am worried about the taxes

Transfer assets into trust → Equipment is sold → Proceeds are invested → Interest is distributed annually → Remaining assets pass to charity at death

The remaining assets must pass to a charity at your death, so additional planning may be needed to ensure you do not disinherit your heirs.

This is a hypothetical example and is not intended to predict or anticipate the actual result of any tax strategy.

Here's how this works:

1. **Assets are placed into a trust**
2. **Equipment is sold:** The first step involves selling the equipment through an auction.
3. **Proceeds are invested:** The money obtained from the sale is then invested.

4. **Interest is distributed annually:** The interest earned from these investments is distributed on an annual basis, potentially providing a steady income stream.
5. **Remaining assets pass to charity at death:** Upon death, the remaining assets in the trust are transferred to a designated charity.

It's crucial to ensure that this strategy doesn't unintentionally disinherit your heirs. Additional planning may be required to balance the interests of your heirs with your charitable intentions.

KEY TAKEAWAYS

- There are two tax codes: one for those who are informed and the other for the uninformed. Both are legal.
- Make sure to understand the four basic rules of all expenses.
- Fire your worst business partner: the tax collector.
- Make sure you are utilizing the Magic Line on your tax return.
- Are you working with a tax preparer or a tax strategist?

LET'S GO DEEPER

If you haven't done so already, go to liveliferichbook.com to get all the documents and graphics in this chapter so you can have a better understanding and overview of your taxes. Be sure to use the questions provided to find out whether you are working with a tax preparer or a tax strategist. Remember, every dollar paid in taxes is a dollar less for your long-term plans and dreams.

8

Will You Pass On a Mess or a Masterpiece?

The Vanderbilt family, led by Cornelius Vanderbilt in the nineteenth century, was once among the wealthiest in America, primarily due to their successful endeavors in shipping and railroads. Cornelius, also known as "Commodore," built a vast fortune that was one of the largest in American history.[12] He provided the initial gift to found Vanderbilt University in Nashville, Tennessee, which is still regarded as one of the top universities in the United States.

However, within just a few generations of his death, the vast wealth of the Vanderbilt family had been significantly depleted. The heirs of Cornelius Vanderbilt were known for their lavish spending on mansions, parties, and other luxuries rather than investing in or growing the family's business interests. By the mid-twentieth century, much of the Vanderbilt family's wealth evaporated. None of the descendants had Cornelius's business prowess, and many of the family's mansions were eventually sold off, demolished, or donated to preservation societies due to the high cost of maintenance and (yep, you guessed it) taxes.[13]

The Vanderbilt story serves as a classic example of how wealth, when not managed with foresight and intention, can be squandered within just a few generations. It highlights the importance of not only building wealth but also educating the following generations on how to manage and sustain it.

THE REAL HEART OF ESTATE PLANNING: YOUR FAMILY MISSION STATEMENT

Estate planning starts with having a plan for your estate. What are the values you want to pass down? What is the culture of your family? What do you want to set the tone for, now that you've worked so hard to build your business and pass it on to the next generation?

Thinking through the values of your family and legacy is a lost art. Family crests, also known as coats of arms, were symbols of pride and identity for noble families in medieval Europe. They often featured animals, plants, colors, and other symbols that represented the family's heritage, achievements, and values. Family crests served as a visual representation of a family's history and lineage, and they adorned shields, banners, seals, and other objects serving as a mark of honor. The tradition of family crests has faded in modern times, though now I'm thinking about having my family design one! My point here is, be intentional with your family about identifying the values you hold dear.

One of the ways my family does that is through weekly spaghetti dinners. It's a tradition we still swear by not just because my sauce is good (hint: I put a bit of brown sugar in it) but because of the memories we've shared at the table. Everyone is welcome, whether they're family, friends, or acquaintances passing through. We've hosted everyone from my kids' friends to foreign dignitaries. Slurping down pasta and swapping stories has become a kind of road map that guides us in our daily lives and reflects our values and priorities.

If it's too difficult to get everyone together for something once a week or you're already living some distance away from loved ones, consider using your cell phone to create something truly meaningful. Record a video or jot down on paper your thoughts, your values, the things you cherish and believe in. I've heard of several parents who write emails to a secret email account that they'll release the username and password to when their kids turn eighteen. Start your message with something like, "The greatness I see in you is . . ." and go from there. Highlight their strengths, encourage them, and inspire them.

These are all creative ways to set a tone for future generations, saying, "Here's what our family values are; here's our story." Or simply recognize and appreciate the greatness within your family members. A very cool trend I've seen in the lives of my clients (in lieu of family crests) is the family mission statement. Here are a few samples you might be able to take and tweak for your own use:

- "In the Johnson family, we cherish honesty, kindness, and hard work. We commit to supporting each other's dreams, celebrating our successes, and learning from our failures. We strive to contribute positively to our community and to treat all people with respect and empathy. Our home is a place of love, laughter, and learning, where each member is valued and heard."
- "As the Patel family, we uphold the values of education, perseverance, and cultural heritage. We believe in the power of unity, respecting our elders, and nurturing our children. Our mission is to create a legacy of community service, maintain strong family bonds, and honor our ancestral traditions while embracing modern progress."
- "Together as the Nguyen family, we embrace adventure, curiosity, and creativity. We encourage individuality and freedom of expression, balanced

with a strong sense of responsibility and integrity. We are committed to environmental stewardship, lifelong learning, and fostering a safe and inclusive home environment."
- "The Smith family is dedicated to living with compassion, integrity, and resilience. We believe in the importance of health—both mental and physical—and in the joy of simplicity and gratitude. Our goal is to support each other unconditionally, to make a positive impact in our community, and to cherish every moment together."
- "In the Garcia family, we value faith, love, and perseverance. We are committed to nurturing strong family ties, celebrating our diverse backgrounds, and providing a supportive environment for personal growth. Our mission includes giving back to our community, living sustainably, and ensuring that every family member feels valued and empowered."

Peter Lynch, a highly respected and renowned former mutual fund manager, once said, "Know what you own, and know why you own it." Whether you're thinking about selling your business someday or handing it over to your kids, there are huge lessons that can be passed on to them that flow simply from you being an entrepreneur. It's the kind of learning they can't get anywhere else.

It's not just about making money. It's about doing something meaningful, making a difference, and standing strong. That's what we're really passing on—a legacy that's more about who you are than what you have.

WHAT HAPPENS IN THE CASE OF THE BIG FIVE?

Back in chapter 5, I shared the story of one of my clients who had a booming business but got sick. It could have been worse, and for many families it is. I've seen way too many situations where a family is left with a mess rather than a masterpiece after a business is passed on.

It's imperative that you prepare for these big five contingencies:

1. Death
2. Disability
3. Disagreement
4. Divorce
5. Retirement

Protection isn't the most glamorous aspect of business, but it's essential. If you have business partners, you need to prepare for the "big five" because every person you partner with creates that much more of a chance that one of those scenarios will present itself to one of you. You need to set things up in a way that allows your business partners and family to handle the unexpected, making sure that both the business and the individuals involved are protected. Let's cover each of these scenarios so that you have some actionable tips in case these come across your path.

DEATH

Death is a topic that many of us would prefer to avoid, yet it's one of life's few certainties. As a business owner, you've poured your heart, time, energy, and probably a few sleepless nights into building something meaningful. But if the unexpected happens, you want to ensure that all your hard work doesn't fall into chaos.

Step 1: Know the Value of Your Business

The first thing your family will need is a clear understanding of what your business is worth. As an entrepreneur, you likely view your business through the lens of years of hard work, sacrifice, and personal investment. However, potential buyers will look at it differently. To them, what matters most is the business's cash flow, systems, and overall viability as an investment.

To simplify this, have a recent business valuation included in your legacy binder (more on this later) or central document. This should cover:

- **Current Market Value:** What's your business worth today?
- **Valuation Methodology:** A summary of how this valuation was calculated (e.g., based on revenue, cash flow, assets).
- **Supporting Documentation:** Financial statements and relevant documents that a prospective buyer would need.

This preparation ensures your family isn't left guessing and can approach potential buyers with a solid understanding of your business's worth.

Step 2: Maintain a List of Potential Buyers

Identifying potential buyers in advance can save your family considerable time and stress. The best candidates often include your current collaborators, competitors, or other stakeholders who understand your industry and would see value in your business.

Within your legacy binder, include:

- **A List of Prospective Buyers:** Collaborators, competitors, or trusted individuals who might be interested.
- **Contact Information:** Make it easy for your family to reach out.

- **Your Preferences:** If you have strong preferences for who should (or should not) take over, document them here.

Knowing who could take over the reins helps your family feel more secure, knowing they're equipped to keep the business running—or sell it to the right hands.

Step 3: Create a Continuity Plan

One of the biggest challenges when a business owner passes away is continuity. If your business relies heavily on you, it may struggle to keep operating smoothly. A continuity plan provides a road map, ensuring that the business can function and continue generating income even if you're not there.

Your continuity plan should include:

- **Standard Operating Procedures (SOPs):** Step-by-step instructions for core business functions.
- **Key Contacts:** Information for essential team members, vendors, and clients.
- **Roles and Responsibilities:** Clear documentation of who does what, so your family or temporary managers understand the key pieces of your business.
- **Cash Flow and Accounts:** Make it clear where funds come from and how expenses are

handled, so operations don't stall due to logistical confusion.

Consider this continuity plan as your business's "life raft." By outlining the necessary steps to keep things moving, you're providing your family and partners with the tools they need to handle the business with care.

Step 4: Assemble a Trusted Team

In the event of your passing, your family will likely need guidance from trusted professionals who can help navigate the complexities of transferring or winding down your business. Here's who you'll want in their corner:

- **Accountant:** To manage finances, tax obligations, and payroll.
- **Attorney:** To handle legal aspects, contracts, and any transfer of ownership.
- **Financial Adviser:** To help guide long-term decisions and ensure the business assets are managed wisely.
- **Business Coach or Consultant:** For industry-specific insights and strategic guidance during the transition.

List these professionals along with their contact information in your legacy binder. This team can help your family avoid costly mistakes and protect the value you've worked so hard to build.

Step 5: Prepare a "Death Checklist" for Your Family

Losing a loved one is hard enough without adding a mountain of logistics. By creating a simple checklist of immediate steps, you can make this difficult time a bit easier for those you leave behind. Here's an example of what this checklist could look like:

1. **Notify Key Contacts:** Inform your accountant, attorney, financial adviser, and business coach.
2. **Gather Financial Documents:** Access recent financial statements, tax records, and valuation documents.
3. **Contact Prospective Buyers:** Start the conversation with your pre-identified list of buyers, if applicable.
4. **Implement the Continuity Plan:** Follow the SOPs to ensure daily operations continue smoothly.
5. **Meet with the Trusted Team:** Bring together the accountant, attorney, financial adviser, and business coach to review the transition process.

This checklist should be readily available for your family, allowing them to focus on honoring your legacy rather than scrambling to figure out where to start.

DISABILITY

Life can be unpredictable, and as a business owner, it's essential to plan for scenarios where you may be unable to work temporarily—or even permanently—due to a disability. If illness or injury strikes, you want to ensure that your business continues to thrive and that your personal finances remain stable. You can also apply the insights in this section to a business partner in the event something happens to them.

Step 1: Understand Your Role in the Business

As the business owner, you likely wear many hats, and if you're unable to work, someone will need to step in to cover your responsibilities. Start by clearly outlining the roles you play within the business. Consider:

- **Primary Responsibilities:** What are the core tasks you handle that are essential for the business to operate?
- **Revenue-Generating Activities:** Identify the tasks directly tied to bringing in income, whether it's client acquisition, relationship management, or specific operational tasks.
- **Unique Expertise:** List any specialized knowledge or skills you contribute that may be challenging to replace.

Documenting these details will help clarify what's needed to keep the business functional in your absence and identify the type of person who could take over, either temporarily or permanently.

Step 2: Assess the Cost of Replacing Your Role

Replacing yourself within the business can be a complex task, especially if your role involves specialized skills or knowledge. It's important to assess what it would cost to hire someone to step into your shoes, even if only temporarily. Here's how:

- **Market Rate Analysis:** Research the going rate for your role, whether that's as CEO, lead sales generator, or subject-matter expert.
- **Skill-Level Requirements:** Identify the skill set required and the potential increase in compensation for specialized or senior-level expertise.
- **Budget Considerations:** Determine if the business can afford a temporary or permanent replacement at the needed salary level, and explore options such as adjusting the role's scope or dividing responsibilities among current team members.

Knowing the real cost of replacing your role can help you budget appropriately and set expectations for your team and family if you're ever unable to work.

Step 3: Protect Your Personal Income

As a business owner, it's crucial to consider what would happen to your personal income if you were to become disabled. Disability insurance can provide a safety net, ensuring you still receive an income to support yourself and your family if you're unable to work. Here are a few key points to keep in mind:

- **Disability Insurance:** Invest in a disability insurance policy that covers at least 60–70 percent of your current income. This can help replace your personal income, reducing the financial strain on your family.
- **Short-Term vs. Long-Term:** Decide whether you need short-term disability coverage, long-term coverage, or both. Short-term policies typically cover a few months, while long-term policies can extend for years.
- **Policy Details:** Review the policy's terms carefully to understand waiting periods, coverage limits, and any exclusions. Make sure your policy covers the specific type of work you do and aligns with your income needs.

Having disability insurance in place can make all the difference in maintaining your lifestyle and financial stability during a difficult time.

Step 4: Build a Business Continuity Plan

A business continuity plan is a road map that details how the business will continue operating if you're unable to lead. This plan should cover:

- **Standard Operating Procedures (SOPs):** Create clear, documented processes for all essential business functions. This way, a temporary replacement can step in and follow established steps without confusion.
- **Key Roles and Backups:** Identify the key roles within your business and assign backup team members who can handle responsibilities in case of an emergency.
- **Financial Contingencies:** Make sure the business has enough reserves or credit lines to cover unexpected expenses, like hiring temporary staff or adjusting operations during your absence.
- **Communication Plan:** Decide who will communicate with clients, vendors, and partners in the event of your disability, ensuring they're aware of any temporary changes in leadership or contact points.

This continuity plan helps ensure that your business doesn't skip a beat, maintaining operations and revenue even if you're sidelined.

Step 5: Establish an Agreement with Business Partners

If you have business partners, it's essential to have a clear agreement in place that outlines what happens if one of you becomes disabled. This agreement should cover:

- **Buyout or Earn-Out Options:** Decide if the disabled partner will be bought out over time or if they'll continue to receive distributions as an investor. Outline the terms to avoid misunderstandings or financial strain on the remaining partners.
- **Role Transition:** Clarify how the disabled partner's responsibilities will be covered, whether by a hired replacement, existing team members, or a shift in duties among the remaining partners.
- **Timeline and Review Process:** Agree on how long the business can operate with a disabled partner before a permanent solution is needed. This prevents undue burden on other partners and provides a clear transition plan.

Partners need to have open, honest conversations about these potential scenarios, ensuring that everyone's expectations are aligned. Clear agreements protect both the disabled partner's interests and the operational stability of the business.

Step 6: Create a Checklist for Disability Preparedness

Finally, create a checklist of immediate steps that your family or business partners can follow if you become disabled. This checklist should include the following steps:

1. **Notify Key Contacts:** Ensure your accountant, attorney, and business coach are informed.
2. **Access Financial Reserves:** Identify which accounts or credit lines can be tapped to support the business if revenue is affected.
3. **Initiate the Continuity Plan:** Follow the SOPs and activate backup roles as outlined in the continuity plan.
4. **Review Insurance Coverage:** Check the status of any disability insurance policies and confirm when benefits will begin.
5. **Meet with Trusted Advisers:** Your family or partners should meet with your core team (accountant, attorney, financial adviser, business coach) to discuss next steps and ensure the business remains on track.

Disability is a challenging reality that no one hopes for but everyone should prepare for. By taking these steps, you're building a resilient foundation for your business and securing your family's financial future. Whether you're out for a short time or permanently unable to return, your business can continue to thrive—and your loved ones won't be left wondering how to pick up the pieces.

DISAGREEMENT

In business partnerships, disagreements are almost inevitable. Two (or more) minds working toward a shared goal will naturally have differences in opinions, approaches, and strategies from time to time. When managed well, these differences can lead to growth and innovation. But if they're left unresolved or allowed to escalate, disagreements can harm the business, strain relationships, and even threaten the partnership itself.

Planning for the possibility of a major disagreement is an essential step in preserving your business's stability and longevity. By putting a clear framework in place, you're preparing to navigate conflicts constructively, ensuring that any disagreements lead to healthy resolutions rather than long-lasting issues.

Step 1: Define Roles and Responsibilities

The foundation of a healthy partnership starts with clearly defined roles. By establishing who is responsible for what, you reduce the risk of stepping on each other's toes. This means:

- **Clarifying Decision-Making Authority:** Decide which decisions each partner has the authority to make independently and which require joint agreement. For instance, maybe one partner handles operational choices, while the other focuses on strategic direction.
- **Outlining Boundaries:** Set clear boundaries to avoid overlapping responsibilities that could lead to conflict. For example, if one partner is responsible for sales, the other should respect that territory and avoid involvement unless requested.
- **Documenting Duties:** Put these roles and responsibilities in writing. When things are clearly documented, it's easier to prevent misunderstandings and address any issues quickly.

These steps help prevent disagreements from arising due to misaligned expectations or unintentional overstepping.

Step 2: Establish a Dispute Resolution Process

Disagreements are natural, but without a plan for how to handle them, they can become disruptive. Set up a clear dispute resolution process that outlines the steps you'll follow to work through any conflicts. Consider including:

- **Open Dialogue:** Agree to discuss disagreements openly and calmly, focusing on facts rather than emotions. Schedule regular check-ins to discuss ongoing concerns and ensure that small issues don't fester.
- **Mediation Options:** Identify a neutral third party, such as a business coach or trusted adviser, who can step in as a mediator if you reach an impasse. Mediation can help defuse tension and guide both sides toward a fair resolution.
- **Escalation Path:** Define when and how issues should be escalated if they cannot be resolved at the partner level. This might involve bringing in a professional mediator or seeking legal advice.

Having a resolution process in place keeps conflicts from spiraling and gives each partner confidence that disagreements can be resolved fairly and professionally.

Step 3: Consider My Approach—"Don't Partner with What You Can Buy"

I believe in partnering only when it's truly beneficial. A key piece of advice: *Don't partner with what you can buy.* Partnerships should be reserved for strategic, long-term collaborations where each party brings unique value that cannot simply be purchased or outsourced. For example:

- **Assessing Core Needs vs. Extras:** Before considering a partnership, ask yourself if what you're seeking could be easily bought or subcontracted. If so, it may not be worth the added complexity and potential for disagreements that come with formal partnerships.

- **Valuing Independence:** Retaining control over key elements of your business is often preferable to relying on a partner, especially for skills or resources you could get in other ways. Partnering with someone just to gain access to something that could be bought often complicates things unnecessarily and may lead to conflict over time.

- **Ensuring Mutual Contribution:** True partnerships are built on mutual contribution and aligned vision. I encourage you to be discerning, focusing on partnerships where both parties are equally invested and essential to the mission. This approach not only protects against potential conflict but also allows both parties to focus on growth and innovation.

By following this principle, you're more likely to find partners who are essential collaborators rather than conveniences. This ensures that any partnerships you enter into are meaningful, sustainable, and valuable to both parties.

Step 4: Value the Business with a "Buy-Sell" Agreement

Sometimes, partners may reach a fundamental disagreement that neither side is willing to compromise on, and it's best for both parties to part ways. A buy-sell agreement provides a structured way to navigate this possibility. This agreement should cover:

- **Business Valuation:** Outline the methodology for valuing the business if one partner wants to exit. Agreeing on a valuation approach in advance prevents disputes over the company's worth.
- **Buyout Terms:** Decide whether a buyout will be a lump sum or an earn-out over time. Include specifics such as payment schedules, interest rates (if applicable), and any terms related to seller financing.
- **Triggering Events:** Specify events that could trigger a buyout, such as a significant disagreement, breach of contract, or other circumstances that indicate it's time for one partner to exit.

A well-structured buy-sell agreement offers peace of mind, providing each partner with a clear path forward if they decide it's best to end the partnership.

Step 5: Align on Long-Term Vision and Values

One of the main sources of tension in partnerships is a misalignment on long-term vision and core values. Take time to align on your overall vision and shared values, as these serve as a compass for the business. Key areas to discuss include:

- **Growth Goals:** Are you both on the same page about the scale and speed of growth? One partner may prioritize rapid expansion, while the other prefers steady, sustainable growth. Clarify these preferences and agree on a path forward.
- **Core Values:** Identify and agree on your business's core values. These values should guide your actions and decision-making, providing a solid foundation that both partners can rally around.
- **Exit Strategy:** Discuss the long-term plan for the business. Do both partners envision staying for the long haul, or is one partner considering an exit in the near future? Understanding each other's goals can help prevent surprises down the line.

Alignment on vision and values strengthens your partnership, making it easier to resolve conflicts by focusing on shared goals and common ground.

Step 6: Prepare a Checklist for Handling Disagreements

Creating a checklist for handling disagreements can simplify the process and ensure that conflicts are managed consistently and constructively. Your checklist might include:

1. **Pause and Reflect:** Take a moment to gather your thoughts before addressing any disagreements, ensuring that emotions don't cloud your judgment.
2. **Schedule a Meeting:** Set aside dedicated time to discuss the disagreement, with a focus on finding a solution rather than assigning blame.
3. **Stick to the Facts:** Approach the discussion with a fact-based perspective, avoiding personal criticism and focusing on the business impact.
4. **Consider All Perspectives:** Actively listen to your partner's point of view, acknowledging their concerns and striving to find common ground.
5. **Bring in a Mediator (If Needed):** If you're unable to resolve the disagreement on your own, involve a trusted third party to help guide the conversation.

By following this checklist, you can approach disagreements in a structured, objective way, making it more likely that you'll reach a resolution that respects both partners' perspectives.

Building a Partnership That Lasts

Preparing for disagreements might feel a bit uncomfortable, but it's a crucial step in building a resilient, lasting partnership. By defining roles, establishing a dispute resolution process, choosing partnerships wisely, creating a buy-sell agreement, and aligning on values, you're proactively reducing the potential for conflict. And if a major disagreement does arise, you'll have the tools and framework to address it head-on, keeping your business on course.

Remember, a strong partnership is built on trust, communication, and shared goals. By preparing for the hard conversations up front, you're investing in a smoother, more harmonious journey together.

DIVORCE

Divorce is one of the most challenging life events to navigate, and when a business partnership is involved, it can introduce additional complexities. Even if the divorce doesn't directly involve your business partner, it can affect the business itself. Emotions are high, financial stakes are involved, and legal entanglements may come into play. Preparing for this scenario ahead of time helps protect your business and ensures that all parties involved can find a path forward without unnecessary disruption.

Step 1: Plan for a "Triggering Event" in Your Partnership Agreement

When setting up your partnership, include divorce as a triggering event that requires a review of the business agreement. This allows for a structured approach to managing any impacts on the business if one partner goes through a divorce. Specifically, your partnership agreement should cover:

- **Ownership and Buyout Clauses:** Clearly define how ownership interests will be handled if a partner's shares become part of a divorce settlement. This could involve options for the other partner to buy out shares, thereby preventing ownership from passing to an ex-spouse.
- **Limited Control for Ex-Spouses:** Ensure that any ownership interest obtained by an ex-spouse is limited to a financial interest without voting or operational control. This helps keep the business's decision-making process intact, even if ownership becomes partially shared with someone outside the partnership.

Step 2: Include a Fair Valuation Process

Divorce often involves splitting assets, and if your business is one of them, it's super important to have a clear, fair method for valuing the business. This helps avoid disputes about the company's worth and ensures both partners agree on the financial terms up front. Consider:

- **Regular Valuation Updates:** Update your business valuation regularly, ideally every year or two, so that a current and accurate value is always on record. This helps prevent surprises if a divorce occurs and streamlines the process of establishing a buyout or settlement.
- **Neutral Valuation Professional:** Identify a neutral valuation professional in your partnership agreement to assess the business's worth, if needed. A third-party valuation can reduce bias and maintain fairness for both partners, minimizing potential conflicts.

Having a valuation plan in place protects all parties' interests and keeps the business valuation process objective and straightforward.

Step 3: Determine Buyout Terms and Timeline

If a divorce settlement grants partial ownership to an ex-spouse, a structured buyout can prevent the business from becoming entangled in personal disputes. Establish clear buyout terms and timelines in advance, considering options such as:

- **Gradual Buyout:** Set a multiyear buyout schedule to avoid financial strain on the business. This allows the remaining partner to pay the ex-spouse in installments rather than one large lump sum, protecting cash flow and business stability.
- **Immediate Buyout with Insurance:** Consider taking out a life insurance policy that funds a buyout in the event of a triggering event like divorce. This ensures funds are available without impacting the business's finances, making it possible for the remaining partner to regain full control of the business quickly and smoothly.

Structured buyout terms provide peace of mind, helping partners navigate difficult times with minimal impact on the business.

Step 4: Protect the Business's Reputation and Client Relationships

Divorce is a deeply personal, emotional experience. If it affects the business, it's essential to manage how the situation is communicated to clients, employees, and stakeholders to maintain trust and confidence. Here are some best practices:

- **Confidentiality Agreements:** Include confidentiality clauses in your partnership agreement to protect sensitive information about the business.

This helps prevent any private disputes from spilling over into the professional environment.
- **Unified Communication:** If necessary, work together to prepare a unified communication plan to address any inquiries from clients or staff. Even if one partner is going through a difficult time personally, a cohesive message shows stability and professionalism, helping reassure clients that the business remains strong.

Maintaining professionalism and confidentiality protects your business's image, even during challenging personal circumstances.

Step 5: Plan for Temporary Role Adjustments

Going through a divorce is emotionally and mentally demanding, and one partner may need to take a step back temporarily to handle personal matters. Consider building flexibility into your partnership by:

- **Delegating Responsibilities:** Have a plan in place for delegating essential tasks to other team members if a partner needs time away. This ensures the business can continue operating smoothly, even if one partner is less available.
- **Setting Short-Term Agreements:** Include short-term agreements for compensation adjustments if one partner temporarily reduces their

involvement. This keeps the partnership equitable and reduces resentment while allowing for a fair division of responsibilities during difficult times.

Preparing for temporary role adjustments ensures that both partners feel supported while protecting the business's continuity.

Step 6: Keep the Long-Term Vision in Mind

In times of personal upheaval, it's easy to lose sight of the bigger picture. As partners, reaffirm your shared vision for the business and focus on the goals that brought you together in the first place. Take time to revisit the following:

- **Shared Values:** Discuss your shared values as business partners and how you can support each other in maintaining them, even during difficult times. This strengthens your bond as partners and reminds both parties of the importance of the business's mission.
- **Mutual Respect:** Divorce can test the limits of patience and understanding, but maintaining mutual respect goes a long way toward ensuring that your professional relationship remains strong. Support each other with empathy, recognizing the challenges each partner is facing, and

work together to find solutions that uphold your business's integrity.

Focusing on your long-term vision keeps you both aligned, even during times of personal challenge, and helps ensure that the business remains resilient.

Divorce is a difficult event to plan for, but by addressing it up front in your partnership agreement, you're investing in the security and longevity of your business. Thoughtful preparation for this possibility ensures that your business won't become an additional casualty if personal relationships change.

A strong partnership is built on trust, preparation, and mutual support. By planning for potential triggering events like divorce, you're creating a foundation that not only protects the business but also strengthens the partnership through life's inevitable challenges.

RETIREMENT

Retirement is a milestone that many of us look forward to—an opportunity to step back, enjoy the fruits of our labor, and pursue new adventures or simply take it easy. For business owners and partners, however, retirement brings additional considerations. A smooth retirement transition requires thoughtful planning to ensure the business can continue thriving while protecting the retiring partner's interests.

Whether you're looking to fully step away or gradually reduce your involvement, preparing for retirement ensures that your legacy and your business remain strong.

Step 1: Decide Between Legacy or Sale

One of the first questions to consider when preparing for retirement is whether you want to leave your business as a legacy or prepare it for sale. This choice will shape your exit strategy:

- **Building for Legacy:** If you envision passing your business on to a family member, a key employee, or someone within your organization, start grooming them for leadership early on. This allows them to grow into the role and gives you the peace of mind that the company will be in capable hands.
- **Preparing for Sale:** If your goal is to sell the business, focus on making it attractive to potential buyers. This means having strong financials, standardized operating procedures, and a solid team in place. Buyers are often interested in businesses that can run smoothly without heavy reliance on the departing owner.

Deciding between legacy and sale helps you create a road map for retirement that aligns with your personal and financial goals.

Step 2: Identify a Successor (If Building for Legacy)

If you want the business to continue within the family or with a trusted employee, identifying and preparing your successor is essential. This process may include:

- **Training and Mentorship:** Start training your successor well in advance of your planned retirement. Share your knowledge, involve them in decision-making, and offer mentorship so they can gain confidence and experience.
- **Defining Roles:** Transitioning leadership isn't an overnight process. Define clear roles for both yourself and your successor during this period, setting boundaries on when and how responsibilities will shift over time.
- **Testing the Waters:** Let your successor take the lead on some projects or decisions, allowing them to get a taste of full responsibility while you're still available for guidance. This can help ease any fears and ensure they're ready to take the reins.

Preparing a successor ensures that your business's mission and values live on, providing continuity and stability even after you step back.

Step 3: Establish Buyout Terms (If Selling)

For those planning to sell, a structured buyout plan helps protect your financial interests while ensuring a smooth handover. Consider options such as:

- **Earn-Out Agreements:** Small-business buyers may not have the capital to pay a large lump sum up front. An earn-out allows the buyer to pay over time, often from the business's profits, which can ease the financial burden on both parties.
- **Partial Buyouts:** If you're not ready to fully retire, a partial buyout allows you to retain some ownership while passing the majority to the buyer. This option lets you stay involved on a limited basis, providing continuity without the full responsibility of running the company.
- **Immediate Sale:** If you prefer a complete, immediate sale, prepare your financials, legal documents, and any necessary transfer agreements to make the process as seamless as possible.

Clear buyout terms protect your retirement funds and provide a straightforward exit path for both you and the buyer.

Step 4: Set Up a Timeline for Transition

Retirement often doesn't happen all at once—it's a gradual process. Establishing a timeline for transitioning out of your business ensures a smooth handover without overwhelming your successor or buyer. Here's a suggested approach:

- **One to Two Years Before Retirement:** Start reducing your involvement by delegating day-to-day tasks and involving your successor in more strategic decisions. This is a time to provide mentorship and build confidence in the new leader.
- **Final Year:** Fully transition major responsibilities and decision-making power. Take a consultant role or remain available for questions, but allow your successor or buyer to fully lead. By the end of this period, the business should be able to run without your input.

A well-planned timeline reduces stress for everyone involved and helps ensure the business continues to thrive.

Step 5: Ensure Financial Security for Your Retirement

Retirement planning is about more than stepping away from day-to-day operations; it's about securing your financial future. Review your retirement plan to ensure it aligns with your lifestyle and financial needs:

- **Maximize Personal Savings:** Supplement any buyout income with personal savings, retirement accounts, and investments to create a solid financial foundation. Make sure your retirement funds are diversified and sufficient for your long-term needs.
- **Insurance and Health Coverage:** Plan for health-care expenses by securing the necessary insurance or health coverage, especially if your current benefits are tied to your business.
- **Contingency Fund:** Build a contingency fund for unexpected expenses or market fluctuations. Having this financial buffer can provide peace of mind and protect your retirement lifestyle.

Financial security in retirement allows you to enjoy your post-business life without the need to reenter the workforce unexpectedly.

Step 6: Define Your New Role (If Any)

Retirement doesn't have to mean a complete separation from the business. Many business owners choose to remain involved in a limited capacity, offering consulting or taking on an advisory role. If this sounds appealing, consider:

- **Consulting or Advisory Role:** Offer your expertise as a consultant, helping with strategic decisions or serving as a sounding board for the new leadership. This allows you to stay connected without the demands of daily operations.
- **Board Membership:** Some retired business owners transition to a seat on the board, providing guidance and continuity. This is a more formal role with defined responsibilities and can be a rewarding way to stay involved.
- **Complete Step-Back:** If you're ready to fully let go, communicate this clearly with your successor or buyer. Leaving the business completely allows you to embrace new opportunities and fully enjoy your retirement.

Defining your role after retirement helps set clear boundaries and expectations, making the transition smoother for everyone involved.

Preparing for Retirement: Setting Up Your Business to Thrive

Retirement is a big step, especially for business owners who have invested years of hard work, energy, and vision into their company. Preparing for it thoughtfully ensures that your legacy is protected, your finances are secure, and the business continues to thrive without you. By following these steps—deciding whether you want to pass on the business or prepare it for sale, identifying a successor or buyout plan, establishing a timeline, and ensuring financial security—you're setting yourself and your business up for success.

Retirement should be a time to celebrate your accomplishments and enjoy the freedom you've earned. With the right planning, you can step into this next chapter with confidence, knowing that your business is in good hands and that you've left a positive impact that will endure.

THE LEGACY BINDER

In my home, there's a binder packed with all the key documents and agreements related to my businesses. This includes everything from legal agreements to important account information—you name it. It's a way of saying to my family, "I've got this sorted out for you," especially if something were to happen to me. Use this list to document what's inside:

1. Accordion file containing titles and deeds
2. A checklist for survivors, listing the people who should be visited after a passing, including those who are handling your affairs or involved in your business
3. Copies of legal agreements related to businesses

4. Important account information for business accounts, including bank accounts, investment accounts, and retirement accounts
5. Insurance policies and contact information for insurance agents
6. List of key contacts, including attorneys, accountants, financial advisers, and business partners
7. Instructions for accessing digital assets, such as online accounts, websites, and social media profiles
8. Inventory of business assets, including equipment, inventory, and intellectual property
9. Personal will and estate-planning documents
10. Plan for the continuation or succession of the business, including any agreements or instructions for business partners or successors

Not having a command center for your financial life can create a logistical nightmare for your loved ones in the event of something happening to you. I learned this lesson the hard way.

Back in chapter 1 I told you about my fiancé, James. When James was being airlifted to Minneapolis for emergency surgery, I was on the phone all night with my attorney and two of my employees, rushing to notarize his legal documents before he was given pain medication. James literally had to stay awake and be fully present so he could sign his health-care directive, durable power of attorney, and so forth—at 2:00 a.m. I felt like I failed him. Because we weren't yet married, I didn't think it was any of my business. But when you love someone you take care of them, no matter what.

Trust me, you never want to be in that kind of situation and you never want to put a loved one in that situation either.

ESSENTIAL ESTATE DOCUMENTS

Having these documents in place ensures that your wishes are carried out and your loved ones are taken care of in the event of your death or incapacitation. Here's a breakdown of the documents highlighted:

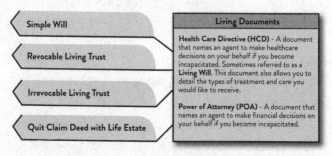

Have you established wills with names and beneficiaries on ALL accounts?

- **Simple Will:** A basic legal document that outlines how you want your assets distributed after your death. It also names guardians for minor children.

- **Revocable Living Trust:** A trust that can be altered or revoked by the grantor during their lifetime. It helps avoid probate and provides privacy regarding the distribution of assets.
- **Irrevocable Living Trust:** Once established, this trust cannot be changed or revoked. It provides tax advantages and protects assets from creditors.
- **Quit Claim Deed with Life Estate:** A legal document used to transfer property ownership while retaining the right to live in the property for the remainder of the owner's life.
- **Health-Care Directive (HCD):** Also known as a living will, this document names an agent to make health-care decisions on your behalf if you become incapacitated. It also allows you to detail the types of treatment and care you would like to receive.
- **Power of Attorney (POA):** This document names an agent to make financial decisions on your behalf if you become incapacitated. It is crucial for managing your affairs if you are unable to do so yourself.

Having these estate documents ensures that your wishes are honored, reduces the burden on your loved ones, and provides clarity and direction during difficult times. It's crucial to establish these documents with named beneficiaries on all accounts to avoid potential disputes and ensure a smooth transition of your assets.

Take the time to review and establish these essential documents as part of your estate planning process. Ensure that your family and loved ones are protected and your wishes are clearly outlined. If you haven't done so already, consult with a legal professional to get these documents in place and regularly review them to keep them up-to-date.

WILLS

A will is the cornerstone of any estate plan, serving as the most basic yet essential document to ensure your wishes are honored after your passing. Let's break down the real purposes of a will:

- **Asset Distribution Instructions:** A will explicitly states how your assets should be distributed among your heirs and beneficiaries. Without these instructions, state laws will determine the distribution, which may not align with your wishes.
- **Personal Representative:** It names a personal representative (or executor) who will manage your estate, ensuring that your instructions are carried out efficiently and accurately.

- **Guardian for Minor Children:** If you have minor children, a will allows you to designate a guardian who will care for them if you pass away, ensuring they are raised by someone you trust.

Assets transferred through a basic will go through a legal process known as *probate*. While probate validates and enforces your will, it comes with its own set of challenges:

1. **Public Knowledge:** Probate makes the details of your asset distribution public. This means anyone can access information about what you owned and who inherits it.
2. **Expense:** Probate can be costly. Attorney fees, court fees, and appraisals can consume 2 to 10 percent of your estate's value, reducing the amount your heirs receive.
3. **Time:** The probate process can be lengthy, often taking six months to a year or more to complete. This delay can cause financial strain and prolonged uncertainty for your loved ones.

Having a will is crucial, but it's also important to understand its limitations and the implications of probate. For many, additional estate-planning tools like trusts may provide more privacy, save on costs, and speed up the transfer of assets.

By addressing these aspects, you ensure your estate plan is comprehensive and tailored to protect your family's future effectively. OK, let's now look at trusts.

TRUSTS

Trusts are a powerful tool in estate planning, offering more control over your assets than a basic will. There are two main types of trusts: revocable and irrevocable.

Revocable Trusts:

- **Flexibility:** Revocable trusts can be altered or revoked at any time, giving you the freedom to change the terms as your circumstances or wishes evolve.
- **Restrictions and Protections:** They allow you to set conditions on how and when your assets are distributed to your heirs, ensuring that your assets are used as you intend.
- **Probate Avoidance:** Assets placed in a revocable trust can bypass the probate process, saving time and reducing costs.
- **Bloodline Preservation:** They can help ensure that your assets remain within your family, protecting them from being misused or claimed by outsiders.

Irrevocable Trusts:

- **Permanence:** Once established, irrevocable trusts cannot be altered or revoked. The decisions made are final, providing a strong level of certainty and security.
- **Restrictions and Protections:** Like revocable trusts, they can set conditions for asset distribution, but with the added benefit of being more secure from changes.
- **Probate Avoidance:** Assets in an irrevocable trust also avoid probate, offering the same benefits of saving time and reducing costs.
- **Bloodline Preservation:** These trusts are effective in keeping assets within the family, providing robust protection for your heirs.
- **Long-Term Care Protection:** Irrevocable trusts can also provide protection for long-term care needs, ensuring that your assets are used to support your future health requirements.

Understanding the differences between revocable and irrevocable trusts is crucial for effective estate planning. Each type of trust serves a different purpose and offers unique benefits.

Revocable trusts offer flexibility and control, making them ideal for individuals who may need to adjust their plans over time.

Irrevocable trusts, on the other hand, offer security and protection, ideal for those looking to solidify their plans and protect their assets from changes and potential liabilities.

LIVING DOCUMENTS

As mentioned earlier this chapter, two crucial "living documents" play an essential role in your estate planning: the power of attorney (POA) and the health-care directive (HCD). These documents ensure that your financial and health-care decisions are managed according to your wishes if you become incapacitated.

Power of Attorney (POA):

- **Role:** The POA authorizes a trusted person, known as an agent, to make financial decisions on your behalf if you are unable to do so.
- **Importance:** This document is crucial for maintaining your financial well-being and ensuring that bills are paid, investments are managed, and financial affairs are in order when you can't handle them yourself.

Health-Care Directive (HCD):

- **Role:** The HCD, sometimes referred to as a living will, designates an agent to make health-care decisions for you if you become incapacitated.
- **Importance:** This document allows you to specify the types of medical treatment and care you wish to receive, ensuring that your health-care preferences are respected even when you can't communicate them.

Having a POA and an HCD in place is about more than just legal preparedness; it's about peace of mind for you and your loved ones. These documents:

1. **Ensure Your Wishes Are Followed:** Both the POA and HCD guarantee that your decisions align with your values and desires, even if you can't voice them yourself.
2. **Prevent Family Disputes:** Clear directives can help prevent conflicts among family members about your care and financial management.
3. **Provide Continuity:** These documents ensure that your financial and health-care matters are handled smoothly, avoiding potential disruptions during critical times.

By establishing these living documents, you take proactive steps to safeguard your future and provide clarity and security for those who may need to make decisions on your behalf.

LIFE REVIEW

A life review is a comprehensive analysis of your current insurance coverage. It helps determine if your policies are performing as intended and still meeting your insurance needs. This review considers any changes in your life circumstances or the insurance industry that might affect your coverage.

Why do you need a life review?

- **Changes in Financial Environment:** The financial environment and the insurance industry are constantly evolving. These changes can impact the effectiveness of your policy.
- **Policy Performance:** It's important to regularly check if your policy is still performing as you intended when you first took it out.
- **Coverage Adequacy:** Over time, your insurance needs may change. A life review ensures that you have the correct amounts and types of coverage to protect yourself and your loved ones.

WHAT DOES A LIFE REVIEW TELL YOU?

- **Continue with Your Current Plan:** If everything is performing as expected and meeting your needs, you can continue with your current plan.
- **Adjust Your Current Plan:** If there are gaps or issues, adjustments may be necessary to ensure your coverage remains effective.
- **The Good, the Bad, the Ugly:** A life review provides an honest assessment of your current coverage, highlighting what's working well, what needs improvement, and any critical issues that need to be addressed.

Regular life reviews are essential for maintaining the relevance and adequacy of your insurance policies. Without these reviews, you risk having outdated or insufficient coverage, which can leave you vulnerable.

LIFE INSURANCE

There are two types of life insurance and a few subcategories.

- **Permanent Life Insurance:**
  - **Whole Life:** Provides lifelong coverage and includes a savings component, where cash value can grow over time.

- **Universal Life:** Offers more flexibility in premium payments, death benefits, and the potential to build cash value based on market performance.
- **Temporary Life Insurance:**
  - **Term Life:** Provides coverage for a specific period (e.g., ten, twenty, or thirty years). It's typically less expensive than permanent life insurance and is ideal for temporary needs.
  - **Credit Life:** Pays off a specific debt if the borrower dies, ensuring that the debt does not pass on to the heirs.

Five Essential Questions to Ask About Your Life Insurance:

1. Do I have a temporary or a permanent need for life insurance?
   - Understanding the duration of your life insurance needs helps you choose between term and permanent policies.
2. How long will my current coverage last?
   - Knowing the term length or the expected duration of your coverage ensures that you are adequately protected for the necessary period.
3. Do I have a current illustration to age one hundred?

- For permanent life insurance, it's crucial to have an updated policy illustration that shows how your coverage and benefits are projected to perform over your lifetime, potentially up to age one hundred.
4. Who are my beneficiaries?
    - Regularly reviewing and updating your beneficiaries ensures that your life insurance proceeds go to the intended recipients.
5. Who owns the policy?
    - Clarifying ownership is essential for understanding who has control over the policy and the associated benefits.

Having the right type of insurance and keeping it up-to-date ensures that your loved ones are protected and your financial legacy is secure. By asking these key questions, you can better navigate your life insurance options and make informed decisions that align with your long-term goals and needs.

WHAT IS YOUR BUSINESS CONTINUITY PLAN?

The business continuity plan is your road map for navigating unexpected challenges or disruptions that could impact the operation and sustainability of your business. It ensures the continuity of business operations and minimizes potential risks and losses in the face of unforeseen events.

Key components of the business continuity plan include:

- **Buy-Sell Agreement:** This is a legally binding contract that outlines what will happen to a business in the event of a triggering event, such as the death, disability, or retirement of an owner. It typically details how ownership interests will be transferred or sold and at what price.
- **Key Person Insurance:** This is insurance coverage taken out on key individuals within the business whose sudden absence or incapacity could have a significant impact on the company's operations and profitability. The proceeds from the policy can help offset financial losses and cover expenses during a transition period.
- **Chain of Command:** This means clearly defining who will be responsible for making critical decisions and managing day-to-day operations in the absence of key personnel. It's essential to identify backup individuals who can step in and fill crucial roles to ensure business continuity.
- **Natural Disaster Preparedness:** It's imperative to develop plans and protocols to mitigate the

impact of natural disasters—such as hurricanes, earthquakes, or floods—on your business operations. This may involve implementing emergency-response procedures, securing backup facilities, and safeguarding critical data and assets.
- **Death or Disability Planning:** Prioritize establishing protocols and contingency plans to address the potential loss of key stakeholders due to death or disability. This includes identifying successors, creating a transition plan, and ensuring continuity in leadership and decision-making processes.

By proactively addressing these elements and incorporating them into your business continuity plan, you can enhance the resilience of your business and better position yourself to navigate unforeseen challenges and disruptions effectively.

It doesn't matter whether you're building to sell or building for legacy to pass a business on to your family. You must be prepared for the inevitable day that you'll be gone. In this case, how you leave one season determines how your loved ones enter the next. Let's not pass on a mess; let's pass on a masterpiece.

KEY TAKEAWAYS

- Estate planning starts with having a plan for your estate.
- Consider drafting a family mission statement, or record a video and tell loved ones how meaningful they are to you.
- Make sure you understand and prepare for the Big Five: death, disability, disagreement, divorce, and retirement.
- "Know what you own, and know why you own it."
- How you leave one season determines how you enter the next.

LET'S GO DEEPER

If you haven't done so already, go to liveliferichbook.com to get all the documents and graphics in this chapter so you can have a better understanding and overview of your legacy pieces.

9

13 Money Habits to Create Wealth

In the world of business there is a very real connection between personal financial habits and business success. In my decades of work in financial planning, it's been rare to encounter someone who excels in managing business finances while their personal finances are a mess.

However, earning money is just one part of the equation. Keeping it and growing it is another ball game. It's hard to outearn poor financial habits. According to a 2009 *Sports Illustrated* article, about 60 percent of NBA players go broke within five years of leaving the game.[14] Just because you're world-class in something and make a lot of money doing it (in this case, basketball) doesn't mean you're world-class with your money or you'll retire rich.

I've been privileged enough to work with a lot of wealthy people over the years and can tell you that there is no real secret to money. It takes years of hard work, with many little smart decisions over time. Let's look at a few of the things I've noticed and use these as a springboard to develop a stronger money mindset.

1. CREATE A BUDGET OR CASH-FLOW PLAN

Let's start with the first and one of the most fundamental habits: creating a cash-flow plan, or in simpler terms, a budget. Knowing where your money is going is crucial.

You don't need anything fancy for this. Just grab a notebook from your local store and jot down everything. Look at your bank and credit card statements. What are you really spending each month? Is it $1,300, $2,500, or maybe $10,000?

Once you have that figured out, balance your income with your expenses. This exercise, as basic as it might seem, is one of the healthiest financial habits you can develop.

Know your numbers. Always.

2. PAY GOD FIRST

This principle was instilled in me since my Sunday school days and involves giving back 10 percent of whatever I get. You might call it a donation or something else, but in my life I call it a tithe. Whether it's a paycheck or a distribution, a portion of what I make is set aside to make a difference in the world.

After this, pay yourself. Yep, you should be next in line. It's not just about setting aside money for bills or debts; it's about valuing your future enough to save for it. *Aim to put away at least 20 percent of your income for yourself.* This 20 percent should be allocated toward savings and investments, ensuring that your future self is financially secure. This could include emergency funds, retirement accounts, and other investment vehicles that will grow over time and provide financial stability.

3. BUCKET LIST YOUR CASH

Remember the three buckets we discussed in chapter 5 (short-term, intermediate, and legacy)? The short-term bucket is for immediate or near-future needs. The intermediate bucket is tax-deferred until retirement and and contains money you won't need for three to ten years. Finally, the long-term bucket (also called the legacy bucket) is for long-term planning and goals.

When it comes to investing your money, there are also three places you can invest: your own business, other people's businesses, and real estate.

4. SET SPECIFIC FINANCIAL GOALS

Without a goal, your savings will just drift along without purpose. Even a dead fish can go with the flow. Set specific financial goals and keep finding reasons to pursue them, even fun ones like the things you listed on your bucket list.

Growing up, vacations were just a dream for me. One of my biggest goals was to change that for my kids. Whether it was saving up for a toy when my kids were first born or taking my daughter on a tour through Europe, I found reasons to stay on course and accomplish certain goals. I plastered pictures of what I wanted everywhere—on my fridge, by my desk—constant reminders of what I was working toward.

5. PAY OFF YOUR CREDIT CARDS

I'm not one of those folks who thinks you should never use credit cards. I use my Delta card for everything because I love the SkyMiles perks, but I make sure it's paid off every single month. Paying off your credit cards regularly is a big step toward financial freedom.

Understanding the difference between good and bad debt can be a real lifesaver. Bad debts, like carrying a balance on your credit card, can feel like a tightening noose around your neck. Pay down your cards and keep the balance under control.

6. START AN EMERGENCY FUND

The rule of thumb here is to have about three to six months' worth of expenses saved up. Life loves throwing you curveballs and they never come at a convenient time. You know how it is—just when you think you've got everything under control, something breaks down or an unexpected expense pops up. By setting aside three to six months' worth of expenses, you create a buffer that can help you navigate through these challenges without compromising your financial health.

Everyone is different, but for me personally, I need to have this six months' worth of expenses in my checking account. Others would say that's a bit crazy, but I need to feel I can access it immediately in case something comes up. Whatever your preference, stock up your emergency fund.

7. HAVE A RETIREMENT PLAN

What we do in our twenties, thirties, forties, and fifties sets the stage for our sixties and beyond. If you retire at fifty and live to ninety, your money will need to last three more decades. Unfortunately, many people don't start seriously thinking about their wealth until they hit their forties, which often leaves them with only a twenty- to twenty-five-year window to really grow their savings.

We touched on this a bit back in chapter 7. The bottom line: start putting away some of your hard-earned money for your future self. Plant seeds today for the tree you'll sit under tomorrow. Don't worry if you can only start small. Even if it's just ten dollars or twenty-five dollars a week, the important thing is that you start. Building this habit will lead to wealth over time, and your future self will be so grateful.

8. PAY YOUR BILLS ON TIME

Late payments can affect your credit score and limit your financial opportunities down the road. It's not just about avoiding late fees; it's about keeping your financial reputation spotless. Moreover, you want to honor the principle of paying the people you owe on time.

You'd be furious if your employer or client kept paying you late, especially if they had the money. Make sure your energy is at a high vibe and that you are honoring your commitments. The simplest thing to do here is to pair your monthly budgeting with automatic payments. Set up auto-pay for everything from credit cards to your utility bills.

I set most of my bills to be paid either on the second or the sixteenth of each month. This way, I always know that there needs to be enough in my account to cover these bills when their due dates roll around. It's like clockwork and takes a load of worry off my shoulders.

Setting up auto-pay is super easy. Just call up your service providers and ask for an electronic funds transfer (EFT) form to set up automatic payments. This little step can save you a lot of hassle and keep your financial health in tip-top shape.

9. EDUCATE YOURSELF

Eleanor Roosevelt, who I absolutely admire, once said, "It takes as much energy to wish as it does to plan." It's time to shift gears from wishing to planning.

Education is a cornerstone of my success. Every week, I download a new book or podcast to listen to. Every morning, as I'm prepping for my day—doing my hair and trying to make those under-eye bags disappear (which can take a hot minute)—I have an audiobook playing.

Turn your daily routines into opportunities for growth and learning. When an idea or thought sparks something inside you, write it down. Some studies say that you're 70 percent more likely to remember something if you write it down versus if you don't.[15]

10. DON'T SPEND MORE THAN YOU HAVE

World-famous investor Warren Buffett once said, "If you buy things you do not need, soon you will have to sell things you need." Just the other day, I was looking through my closet and was surprised how much clutter I had. I saw a lampshade from a broken lamp on the floor. Because this lampshade was pretty expensive, I kept it with the intent to repurpose it or fix it up. It just hit me that several years earlier, that lampshade was cash. Now it was just sitting on my floor, doing nothing. Our closets tell the story of our spending habits, don't they?

We're more likely to overspend when we lose track of what we actually have. Every item cluttering our space, every unnecessary purchase, is a little bit of your financial freedom chipped away. Before you open your wallet next time, ask if what you're buying is something you truly need. It may just be money that ends up as clutter in your closet.

11. CREATE A POSITIVE MONEY MINDSET

We've all picked up some less-than-helpful beliefs about money through the years. Maybe it was something our parents said, or perhaps a mindset we developed from observing others. These beliefs, these broken systems (or BS, as I like to call them), have a way of holding us back.

For a long time, I was driven by the fear of going back to a life I promised to leave behind. Fear can be a powerful motivator but it can also create a scarcity mindset, where no matter how much we have, it feels like it's never enough. I had to change my money mindset from one of scarcity to one of abundance. In the same way we can change the nature of our relationship with a family member, friend, job, or ourselves, we can change our relationship with money. Take a deeper look into your relationship and ask yourself if there are ways you can relate to it in a healthier way.

12. AVOID IMPULSE SHOPPING

We've all indulged in our own form of retail therapy, and I'm no exception. Sometimes the therapy is cheap (like three cartons of ice cream) and other times it's pricey (like three pairs of shoes). Either way, retail therapy always seems to cost more than just the money I spend.

Impulse shopping is often a sign of something deeper. For me, it directly relates to stress. When the pressure mounts, I find comfort in food, especially ice cream. The initial rush is awesome, but the aftermath? Not so much. Then comes the guilt and realization that I'm not addressing the real issue. After one retail escapade too many I realized: *I know better, so I need to do better.*

I'm nowhere near perfect, but one thing that has helped me is to ask, *What do I really want?* A late-night ice cream binge obviously won't give me the health and vitality I desire. So I choose better.

13. DIVERSIFY YOUR INCOME SOURCES

Earlier in chapter 6 we covered eight streams of income. One thing to add here is to move toward either more income from your passive sources or more passive sources in general.

At the start of this chapter I mentioned that it's hard to outearn poor financial habits. Another twist on this: it's difficult to just earn and grind your way to wealth and financial freedom. Even if you have a high-income business, there will always be a sense that all your eggs are in one basket. Every person I know who has achieved a state of financial freedom has diversified income sources. Remember, *make money your best employee.*

The money habits we've explored in this chapter are designed to build a strong financial foundation, regardless of how much money you have or suddenly come into. They are the building blocks of financial success and security.

As you move forward, keep these habits close, let them guide your financial decisions, and watch as they transform not only your bank account but your entire approach to life.

KEY TAKEAWAYS

- Create a budget or cash-flow plan.
- Pay God first.
- Bucket list your cash.
- Set a specific financial goal.
- Pay off your credit cards.
- Start an emergency fund.
- Have a retirement plan.
- Pay your bills on time.
- Educate yourself.
- Don't spend more than you make.
- Create a positive money mindset.
- Don't impulse shop.
- Put your money to work for you in active and passive income sources.

LET'S GO DEEPER

If you haven't done so already, go to liveliferichbook.com to download the workbook. In it, you'll find the thirteen habits in this chapter. Remember, it's difficult to outearn poor financial habits. Print it out and keep it at your desk or phone to help you stay on track.

The World Needs You Rich

For those of us lucky enough to grow old (it's a privilege), life is a marathon, not a sprint.

We've talked a lot about planning, preparing, and building during our time together. We've cast a vision for the future in business, finances, and life. There's a lot of work to do, and while the work might seem daunting, there's probably a part of you that's excited about rising to the challenge and becoming the person who can turn your dreams into reality.

But the flip side of that coin is that success can often come at the expense of your own sanity. As business owners and entrepreneurs, we can lose ourselves in the hustle, bustle, and grind. We can become wealthy in our bank accounts all while becoming poor in spirit. I often have to remind myself to slow down, look at my life, and focus on *improving* myself instead of just proving myself. When you do, new pathways tend to open up that lead to healing, wholeness, abundance, and purpose in unexpected ways.

A few months after my fiancé James passed away, my good friend Chris called me from Costa Rica and suggested I visit. Like, within the next week.

As much as I like to go out and try new things, spontaneity isn't one of my fortes. Remember, farm life taught me to be a planner. Planning seeps into every part of my life: meals, outfits, to-do lists, and so forth. For vacations I need at least a six-month runway, complete with a detailed itinerary. Going to Costa Rica on such short notice was really out of my comfort zone. I admitted to Chris that I actually could use some quiet time to gather myself and heal after losing James. He said he had just the place, and to my surprise, I was on a flight to Costa Rica a few days later.

Once I landed, even getting to this "place" was an adventure. The roads, if they could even be called that, were an endless series of potholes. After three hours of what felt like being in a blender, my head was pounding. *This better be worth it*, I thought to myself.

Finally, we reached a gate with a guard at the base of a mountain. "Here's where you'll be staying," Chris said. A mountain spa retreat! The grind of getting there disappeared as I started dreaming of a five-star resort. The guard swung the gate open and we started the ascent. By then it was dark out, but I could see from the headlights of our vehicle and a bit of the moonlight that the path was lined with boulders and overhanging vines, like something out of *Jurassic Park*.

When we reached the summit, Chris unloaded my bags and told me that if I needed anything, he and his family were just an hour and a half away. "I'll check on you in five days!" And off he went.

Pump. The. Brakes. An hour and a half? Five days?

At least from what I could see, the accommodations looked all right: there was a good-sized mansion adjacent to a quaint little house, called a *casita*. I looked around for the front desk or concierge, but there was nothing to be found. Eventually, a lovely lady named Linda stepped out to greet me and said I'd be staying in the *casita*.

Then, an unexpected twist. Linda glanced at my luggage and asked, "Where are your supplies?"

Supplies? I brought all my favorite supplies: stilettos, sundresses, swimwear, a few books, and some Cheez-Its and candy bars.

I quickly discovered that my luxurious spa retreat was actually just a solitary house on a mountain in the middle of 1,500 acres of untouched jungle. Forget restaurants and room service, Linda was talking to me about machetes and scorpions! She wished me luck and headed off, leaving me with Tito, the non-English-speaking guard. I thought, *What is it with all these people dropping bombs on me and then just driving off?*

Everything in me wanted to call Chris and give him a talking to, but something told me to embrace the adventure. After getting some sleep, I stepped onto the balcony the next morning and was greeted by a breathtaking view.

Clouds were hovering *below* me. Mountains stretched as far as the eye could see. The green foliage was stunning. It was one of the most beautiful places I had ever been.

Later that day I set off to find the beach. Armed with my newfound survival kit—a Bible, bug spray, and a machete—I hacked through the jungle, which I nicknamed "The Valley of the Shadow of Death," reciting Psalm 23 the whole way.

I finally got to a secluded beach that's usually accessible only by boat. This wasn't nature like a local park; this was raw, rugged nature. Jagged rocks, crashing waves, and lots of critters scampering around on the coarse sand. I was out of my comfort zone, but maybe that's exactly where I needed to be to find a new perspective.

I sat on the beach and drew a circle around me in the sand. I was determined to find the silver lining in this wild adventure, even if it meant facing my fears head-on. The next few days were an emotional roller coaster—from tears to laughter, anger to gratitude, and everything in between.

Interesting things happen when we take the courageous step to be alone. As business owners we're always on the go. It's not a stretch to say that work can be a form of escapism from ourselves. It's a rough cycle: we're overwhelmed and feel alone, but because we're alone we fill our lives with more stuff, which only ends up making us feel more alone.

Oftentimes, we're afraid to find out what's really going on inside our heads or hearts and just cram our calendars with more stuff so we don't have to face anything.

One afternoon I was feeling really alone. While trekking back up the mountain, something incredible happened. Two majestic white stallions appeared and walked up the mountain with me. It was surreal, like a scene straight out of a movie. I'm actually glad I didn't have a camera to capture the experience. It allowed me to be fully present. In that moment, I felt a deep sense of peace and realized, *I am not alone*, and Costa Rica won my heart.

WHAT MUST WE DO TOGETHER THAT WE CAN'T DO ALONE?

At the end of the five days, I was back in civilization having dinner with Chris and some other friends. Chris posed a powerful question to us, "What must we do together that we can't do alone?"

We cast a vision to start a foundation in Costa Rica as well as a sewing school for women. Chris had some connections with local leaders and, long story short, by March 2017 we broke ground on the school.

Like any big initiative, there were tough challenges along the way. One thing we really wanted to do was pave a road out of white rocks so locals could avoid walking knee-deep in mud during the rainy season. We had the supplies, but the weight of the rocks being carried in a truck was too heavy to go up the mountain, so we hoofed it by using wheelbarrows and makeshift tools to lay down the rock.

When the local community saw us working our tails off all while having a great time, they joined in. They brought their tools, wheelbarrows, and, most importantly, their spirit. My daughters, Lexi and Danielle, were right there with me. We turned this project into a family mission to honor James, a man we all dearly loved. I believe he would have been proud of us.

There were a lot of people who told us the sewing school couldn't be built, but I'm glad we didn't listen to them. Nearly everything was a challenge—permits, roads, bathrooms. I even had to learn how to build a septic tank.

But today, in the mountains of the beautiful Guanacaste region in Costa Rica, there is a sewing school for women that has become so much more than a place to learn a craft. It's a beacon of hope and opportunity.

Women come from all around not only to learn sewing but to gain leadership skills, business knowledge, and a sense of empowerment.

That mountain has become a very special place to me. The stars light up the sky in a way that no city lights ever could. Yet you feel more grounded to the earth than walking even the most beautiful of beaches.

I have a dream of inviting entrepreneurs and leaders from all over the world to visit to get away, be with themselves, and find that what they're really looking for stems from within. I've attended thousands of events in my life, from church services to business workshops to personal development rallies that pack arenas. People will travel the world seeking breakthroughs, awakenings, and profound spiritual experiences to be with anyone but themselves.

It's interesting how at all of these kinds of events, we dress up in our Sunday or business "best" for others, all while trying to connect authentically with ourselves. I love dressing up, but it's a funny contrast when you think about it.

Sometimes you need to get lost in a jungle to find your true path.

EMPOWERED PEOPLE EMPOWER PEOPLE

One thing you'll notice about good people who have resources is that they tend to gather around causes and think about how they can move society forward. Starting foundations, launching charity initiatives, and empowering others is just as normal to them as movies and popcorn might be to others.

The conversations are different.

The perspective is different.

The energy is different.

Watch any movie and you'll typically see wealthy people or business folks painted as the villains. This stereotype is not only misleading but also harmful. The reality is that many successful people use their resources and influence for the greater good. They create jobs, drive innovation, and support their communities. They understand that true wealth isn't just about accumulating money but about making a positive impact.

In the very first chapter of this book I said there's a good chance that you're one of my favorite kinds of people because you're an entrepreneur.

You're part of a rare breed. You're the hope of the world. *The world needs you rich.*

So would you make me a promise?

Become as great as you've been called to be. See your success as a platform to uplift others. Mentor those around you. Advocate for the less fortunate. Reshape your understanding of wealth and success and recognize that with great resources comes a great sense of responsibility and purpose.

No, we can't change everyone. We can't change everything. But together we can do more than we can alone.

You may have experienced great loss. Your heart may have been broken; you may have been ripped off, stabbed in the back, dragged through the mud, or simply worn down by the weight of life.

I get it. In Costa Rica, with my heart heavy and my world turned upside down, I came to understand that the way out of my own storms was to make a way for others and help them get out of theirs. The way to heal often involves healing others. The way to wealth, abundance, and purpose is often through helping others step into theirs.

Friend, you're still here. You woke up aboveground, not below it. It's time to dream big again.

May you live life rich.

KEY TAKEAWAYS

- Getting old is a privilege.
- Success can come at the expense of your own sanity.
- Focus on improving yourself, not just proving yourself.
- Interesting things happen when we take the courageous step to be alone.
- Sometimes you need to get lost in a jungle to find your true path.

LET'S GO DEEPER

If you haven't done so already, go to liveliferichbook.com to get all the documents and exercises in the book. While you're here, jot down the answers to these questions:

- What experiences have you said yes to that were initially uncomfortable but led to new breakthroughs?
- What must you do together with others that you cannot do alone?
- In what ways can you make your success a platform for others?

ACKNOWLEDGMENTS

To my dear friend and coauthor, Mike Kim—this book would not exist without you. Thank you for pushing me, encouraging me, and investing hours of your life in my journey to write this guide to help others build their rich lives. You are an incredible guide, human, and friend.

To my children, Alexandra, Gabriel, and Danielle Nehlsen—we are stronger and better together, and each of you inspires me to be a better human, a better model, and to keep my priorities in check. Thank you for keeping me real, reminding me how strong I am, and loving me even when I feel unlovable. You are the greatest events of my life.

To Alfredo Delgado—thank you for teaching me there are good days, great days, and growth days. Thank you for being my sounding board, my partner, and for loving me with all my flaws.

To John C. Maxwell—I could not write my story without including you. You've had such a profound effect on my thinking, self-leadership, and growth; I wouldn't be the person I am today without your thirty years of guidance. I am living proof that your life's work... works.

To my clients—thank you for years of teaching me how to be a better adviser, to make better moves, and to stretch to always provide better answers and solutions. You have made me the problem solver I am today.

Thank you to every audience member, workshop attendee, and friend who has said, "You should write a book; people need to know how to do this." I had to hear it a few thousand times, but I finally listened—thank you for the encouragement to "write your dang book."

To the Enemy of my soul—I've read the last chapter of the book... we win. But every day, for the rest of my life, I'm putting you on notice: I'm going to wake up, charge into hell with my water pistols, and reclaim every dream of every entrepreneur I meet, equipping them with the tools to live in freedom. Sorry, you lost. (OK, I'm not sorry.)

Saying thank you doesn't feel like enough, so I hope you know, in the words of the amazing Woody from *Toy Story*, "You've got a friend in me." I love each and every one of you, and I am eternally grateful. Thank you.

To the light that shines within me, from where all my blessings flow... thanks be to God. You said, "Call to me and I will answer you" (Jeremiah 33:3 NIV), and You have shown up for me in every dark night, every

ACKNOWLEDGMENTS

celebratory moment, and every single day in every way from the moment of my birth. You have been with me.

When I was nine years old Your Spirit told me to get up and face my giants. Your hand has always been on me, protecting me, loving me, guiding me. You are my GPS, and I know that all things work together for good for those who love the Lord and who are called according to His purpose. Thank You for calling me. Thank You for loving me. Thank You for giving me purpose. Thank You for every good, bad, and ugly thing that brought me closer to You. Thank You for my rich life. I will not waste it.

ABOUT THE AUTHOR

Marissa Nehlsen is the founder and CEO of a leading financial firm that has guided clients to extraordinary financial results. Rising from humble beginnings in North Dakota, Marissa developed innovative strategies that have helped her and her clients build multimillion-dollar businesses.

A recognized expert in wealth building and tax strategy, Marissa is also a dedicated philanthropist, speaker, and coach. Connect with Marissa at marissanehlsen.com.

NOTES

1. "Oceans," by Matt Crocker, Joel Houston, and Salomon Ligthelm, on *Zion*, Hillsong UNITED, 2013.
2. "Neurological Effects of Positive Affirmations," Inner Growth Coach, accessed January 23, 2025, https://www.innergrowthcoach.com/neurological-effects-of-positive-affirmations/.
3. Oxford Languages, s.v. "entrepreneur," accessed via Google search on July 22, 2024.
4. "Wannabe," by Spice Girls, produced by Matt Rowe and Richard Stannard, Virgin Records, released as a single on June 26, 1996.
5. *Braveheart*, directed by Mel Gibson (Santa Monica, CA: Icon Productions, distributed by Paramount Pictures, 1995), DVD.
6. "Table 7. Age and Employment Status by Industry, 2020," US Bureau of Labor Statistics, accessed January 23, 2025, https://www.bls.gov/bdm/us_age_naics_00_table7.txt.
7. Warren Buffett, in a letter to the shareholders of Berkshire Hathaway, 1991, https://www.berkshirehathaway.com/letters/1991.html.

NOTES

8. Ivan Misner, "Networking Is More About Farming Than It Is About Hunting," *Ivan Misner* (blog), July 30, 2020, https://ivanmisner.com/networking-is-more-about-farming-than-it-is-about-hunting/.
9. Michael E. Gerber, *The E-Myth Revisited: Why Most Small Businesses Don't Work and What to Do About It* (Harper Business, 2004).
10. Chris McChesney et al., *The 4 Disciplines of Execution: Revised and Updated: Achieving Your Wildly Important Goals* (Simon & Schuster, 2022).
11. Steven Handerson, "What Is Amazon Web Services and Why Is It So Successful?," Investopedia, accessed January 23, 2025, https://www.investopedia.com/articles/investing/011316/what-amazon-web-services-and-why-it-so-successful.asp#:~:text=Amazon%20Web%20Services%20(AWS)%2C,1.
12. Christopher Klein, "Cornelius Vanderbilt," History.com, accessed January 23, 2025, https://www.history.com/topics/19th-century/cornelius-vanderbilt.
13. Natalie Robehmed, "The Vanderbilts: How American Royalty Lost Their Crown Jewels," *Forbes*, accessed January 23, 2025, https://www.forbes.com/sites/natalierobehmed/2014/07/14/the-vanderbilts-how-american-royalty-lost-their-crown-jewels.
14. Pablo S. Torre, "How [and Why] Athletes Go Broke," *Sports Illustrated*, March 23, 2009, https://vault.si.com/vault/2009/03/23/how-and-why-athletes-go-broke.
15. "Climate Change: What Is It and Why Is It Happening?," BBC News, accessed January 23, 2025, https://www.bbc.co.uk/newsround/68104618.